Continuous Bloom

Continuous *Bloom*

Written and photographed by
Pam Duthie

Ball Publishing
Batavia, Illinois, U.S.A.

Ball Publishing
335 N. River Street
Batavia, Illinois 60510
www.ballpublishing.com

Designed by Tamra Bell.

Library of Congress Cataloging-in-Publication Data

Duthie, Pam, 1942–
    Continuous Bloom / written and photographed by Pam Duthie.
      p. cm.
    Includes bibliographical references (p.)
    ISBN 1-883052-23-8 (alk. paper)
    1. Perennials. 2. Color in gardening. I. Title.

  SB434 .D88 2000
  635.9'32--dc21
                                    99-088588

Printed in Hong Kong.
10 09 08 07 06 05 5 6 7 8 9 10 11 12

To the attentive eye each moment of the year has its own beauty, and in the same field it beholds, every hour, a picture which was never seen before, and which shall never be seen again.

—Ralph Waldo Emerson

Contents

Acknowledgments

My thanks to my parents, who, because they *didn't* garden, allowed me to experiment and pick the flowers; my grandfather, who taught me to love dirt; and my children, Ann, Todd, and Laurie, who loved having a mom who thought that everyone should play in the dirt. But I especially want to thank my husband, who has willingly dug up our gardens throughout thirty-six years of marriage, lugged my camera and tripod around to "just one more garden," and encouraged me to start my own business, The Gifted Gardener.

Thanks to the Landscape Design Association, the Perennial Plant Association, and the Chicago Botanic Garden, where I have been able to teach and lecture, synthesize ideas, and get out and see gardens with the perennials included in this book. A special thanks to Richard Hawke (plant evaluation coordinator, Chicago Botanic Garden) for answering all my horticultural questions, no matter how stupid, and to John Brookes, who encouraged me in landscape design to see the "big picture" and to take time to get "the essence of the garden."

My sister and friend Diane McCormick has offered lots of encouragement, gardened with me throughout the years, filed slides, and came up with the "clusters of five major bulbs with five grape hyacinth as marker bulbs" idea described in the interplanting bulbs section of chapter 9. Gardening with a buddy makes the hours and achy back pass in no time at all.

Two of my best "cheerleaders" have been Stephanie Cohen from Pennsylvania and Anne Davidson-McNitt from Wisconsin, who made sure I got in to photograph great gardens in their areas and prodded me along to many lecture opportunities. Thanks to all the friends who never complained that I was always in their garden taking "plant portraits": Sharon Anderson, Susan Beard, Barbara Berend, Candy Cleveland, JoAnna Duensing, Erwin and Yolanda Evert, Terry Hickey, Barbara Miller, Margaret Morris, and Lee Randhava. And thanks to Lee, who is also a great wordsmith and a helpful listener.

And finally, for all the people who have attended my lectures or classes and workshops in my garden— you were the test audience for the ideas in this book!

Introduction:

Achieving Continuous Bloom in the Perennial Garden

Continuous bloom is something every gardener strives for! Browsing through this book with its vivid photographs and instant access to information will help you easily plan a garden that blooms all season long.

Start by choosing perennials that bloom the longest and create a nonstop garden by adding the complimentary plants that will extend the season of interest from March to November and even into winter. With this resource, perennials can be chosen by their different bloom times to flow from one month into the next, while perennials with good foliage color can bridge the gaps between bloom times.

The second key to achieving continuous bloom is to know the perennial palette—how they look, how they perform, and where they grow best. This book presents a palette of 272 outstanding and durable perennials organized by their month and length of bloom; the upper corner of each page is clearly color coded to help you find the month of bloom you're looking for.

The month of bloom generally varies from two to four weeks from north to south in the United States. However, snowdrops blooming in March in northern Illinois may bloom in January in Georgia. Using the month of bloom as a general guideline, you can simply browse the pages or choose a month for which you need a plant idea. And particularly watch for perennials with extended bloom times, which are noted with a clock icon at the top of the page.

Each "plant portrait" is in an easy-to-read format with the following information:

Botanical name: Plants are listed by their botanical names. These names should allow you to buy the plant you want wherever you are, as they are standard names that are in use in the United States, England, South America, or wherever you may find yourself. Though these are supposed to be standardized and fixed, some names do change based on the latest studies of plants and interpretations of their origins. I've

tried to be as accurate as possible in naming the plants. While the names here reflect the latest thinking on each species, do not be surprised if you find a few in the garden center under a different name.

Common name: This is the name you probably grew up calling these plants—unless your family owned a garden center! Common names vary from region to region, so you may learn a new name for a favorite plant. And if you know a plant by a different common name than I have listed, drop me a line and let me know.

Plant type: In addition to the classic perennial category—meaning a flowering plant that dies back to the ground each year and comes back the following year to bloom again—I include bulbs, ferns, ornamental grasses, roses, and shrubs used as perennials. Native plants and herbs are also noted, as well as if a plant is evergreen.

Zone: Using the USDA Zone map for cold hardiness, I chose plants that thrive primarily from Zones 3 to 8. Keep in mind, though, that my experience with the plants in this book has been primarily with my Zone 5, northern Illinois region. I have noted where plants will have problems or do exceptionally well in certain zones.

Flower: Here you'll find descriptions of each flower's color of bloom, shape, habit, and fragrance.

Foliage: I've listed color of foliage, habit (clump forming, cascading, spreading), and texture (lacy, bold, glossy). The importance of foliage cannot be emphasized enough in arranging and combining plants in the garden. Foliage acts as a foil or blender to the flower colors and provides important color and texture in the garden when flowers are not in bloom. And although ferns do not bloom, I have included eight as a necessary part of the "continuous bloom" shade garden—their lacy texture fills in for bloom. A leaf icon at the top of the page will indicate a plant with notable foliage.

Bloom length: The number of weeks that a plant can bloom given optimal growing conditions is key to planning a garden with continuous bloom.

Height and spacing: The height and spacing of plants are essential to the placement of perennials in the garden. Plants must have adequate space to mature. Placement will also affect how effectively plants are displayed.

Light: I've listed the best lighting conditions to achieve optimal plant growth for each perennial. Knowing this will avoid the problems caused by too little or too much sun or shade—scorched leaves, straggly rather than compact growth, and fewer blooms.

Soil: Soil type impacts plant performance. Brief descriptions of different soils are given, and like light conditions, the gardener will soon know if the plant has the best growing medium.

Care: Special care requirements for each plant—such as staking, deadheading, pinching back—can be found here. These basic gardening practices are described more fully at the end of the book. If a plant doesn't need special care, it is simply noted as "easy."

Uses: You can use perennials in myriad ways: formal versus informal, perennial or mixed border, wildflower or prairie, woodland, naturalistic, herb, cottage, and scent or color themes. Additional sophisticated uses are: long-blooming (everyone's favorite), background, architectural accent, structure, filler, edger, weaver or blender, groundcover, screening, fragrance, foliage color, and winter interest.

Propagation: For those interested in increasing their plant collection, you will find a discussion of propagation methods and timing. Some perennials *must* be divided regularly to regenerate the plant.

Problems: Diseases, pests, invasiveness, and the need to stake are problems you must evaluate when siting plants in the garden.

Insider's tips: Additional practical advice is offered on how to care for and prolong the bloom time. Other outstanding or new and promising cultivars may be suggested as well.

Combines with: Creative suggestions for unique combinations of perennials with other plant material are included here.

I think the rest of the book will be equally helpful. Chapter 9 offers hints on how to get your garden winter-ready over the course of November, so you're not racing against the snow after Thanksgiving. You'll even see how leaving some plants up will keep your garden interesting long after New Year's Day. Chapter 10 shows you ways to keep busy gardening during the long winter months—it's never too early to plan for next year! In chapter 11, I share hard-learned gardening tips to make your job easier and to spare your back a few aches throughout the season. Several appendixes give you the information you will want quickly: lists of plant societies and mail-order catalogs, colored foliage, some hosta varieties, and astilbes and daylilies you can grow to extend their season of bloom.

Remembering that practice and experience are the best teachers, don't be afraid to experiment with the perennial palette presented in this book. You will learn from your mistakes and be rewarded with your successes. Perennials are very forgiving and can be moved around until you get it just right! So begin by finding those perennials that have the longest bloom times at the end of the June and July chapters, and have a wonderful time creating your own "continuous bloom" garden.

CHAPTER 1

The Emerging Garden:
Hope Springs Eternal

Eranthis hyemalis
WINTER ACONITE

Plant type:	Bulb, summer dormancy **Zone:** 4–7
Flower:	Bright, lemon-yellow buttercup
Foliage:	Delicate ruff or collar of green leaves just under the flower
Bloom length:	2–4 weeks
Height:	3–5 inches **Width/spacing:** 4 inches
Light:	Part shade **Soil:** Rich, moist
Care:	Soak tubers before planting
Uses:	Heralds spring, woodland edge
Propagation:	Self-sows in ideal conditions
Problems:	Summer dormancy
Insider's tips:	Try to place the bulbs along the edges of paths most often used in the early spring so you don't miss this very early bloomer.
Combines with:	*Galanthus elwesii, Vinca minor, Scilla sibirica, Pulmonaria longifolia* 'Bertram Anderson'

Galanthus elwesii
SNOWDROP

Plant type:	Bulb **Zone:** 3–8
Flower:	Nodding, three-lobed white, bell-like; larger flower than the more common *Galanthus nivalis*
Foliage:	Narrow, upright, linear straps
Bloom length:	8 weeks; Brent Heath (of Brent & Becky's Bulbs, Gloucester, Virginia) reports that in Virginia they start in late fall onward!
Height:	6–8 inches **Width/spacing:** 4 inches
Light:	Shade, part shade **Soil:** Rich, moist, well-drained
Care:	Easy
Uses:	Shaded rock garden, woodland, shade edger
Propagation:	Allow to colonize
Problems:	Summer dormancy; getting out to see them when it still seems like winter!
Insider's tips:	This is reported to be fragrant, but this is one flower I have yet to smell—it's usually too cold for me to get down on the ground and sniff.
Combines with:	*Vinca minor, Asarum europaeum, Asarum canadense, Polemonium reptans, Myosotis sylvatica*

Helleborus orientalis
LENTEN ROSE

Plant type:	Perennial, groundcover **Zone:** 3–8
Flower:	Dusky rose to white, saucer-shaped, and somewhat nodding
Foliage:	Evergreen; leathery divided leaves held in a whorl on upright stems
Bloom length:	8 weeks
Height:	15 inches **Width/spacing:** 12–18 inches
Light:	Shade **Soil:** Rich, moist, well-drained
Care:	Fertilize in early spring; cut back any damaged foliage
Uses:	Woodland or shade garden, groundcover, evergreen, long bloomer
Propagation:	Division in fall; self-sows in right location
Problems:	Control slugs and keep soil improved with composted leaves
Insider's tips:	This is one of the most-asked-about perennials in my garden. Because I leave the flowers on most of the summer, I have many seedlings coming along.
Combines with:	*Myosotis sylvatica, Tiarella wherryi, Anemonella thalictroides, Corydalis ochroleuca, Brunnera macrophylla, Galium odoratum*

Sanguinaria canadensis
BLOODROOT

Plant type:	Perennial, native **Zone:** 3–8
Flower:	White, poppylike flower on red, leafless stems
Foliage:	Round leaf is deeply lobed and is tightly rolled around the flower bud as it emerges in spring.
Bloom length:	2–4 weeks
Height:	3–6 inches **Width/spacing:** 8 inches
Light:	Part shade, shade
Soil:	Average to rich, evenly moist, slightly acidic
Care:	Easy
Uses:	Woodland, naturalistic garden, foliage tapestry
Propagation:	Self-sows; division in fall, although they are difficult to find when dormant
Problems:	Early and short bloom time; summer dormancy
Insider's tips:	The plant gets its common name from the reddish colored root. The sap, which is also red, is very toxic—do not ingest!
Combines with:	*Dryopteris marginalis, Adiantum pedatum, Stylophorum diphyllum, Eranthis hyemalis, Hepatica acutiloba*

Scilla sibirica
SCILLA, SIBERIAN SQUILL

Plant type:	Bulb **Zone:** 2–8
Flower:	Blue, gives a spiked effect
Foliage:	3 to 4 straplike leaves, summer dormancy
Bloom length:	5 weeks
Height:	3–6 inches **Width/spacing:** 4 inches, spreading
Light:	Sun to part shade **Soil:** Average, well-drained
Care:	Plant in fall 3 inches deep
Uses:	Edging, naturalizes, early bloom, blue garden, groundcover
Propagation:	Divide clumps after blooming, spreads rapidly
Problems:	Spreads easily into lawns; summer dormancy
Insider's tips:	As the precursor to spring bulb show, it will eventually colonize to be a blanket of early blue flowers.
Combines with:	*Heuchera* 'Plum Pudding', *Mertensia virginica, Stylophorum diphyllum, Anemonella thalictroides*

CHAPTER 2

April

Daffodils and Wildflowers

Pulsatilla vulgaris
PASQUEFLOWER

Plant type:	Perennial **Zone:** 4–8
Flower:	Wine red, cupped anemone flower with a yellow center and an attractive fuzzy seed head
Foliage:	Gray-green, hairy, and fernlike
Bloom length:	2–3 weeks
Height:	18 inches **Width/spacing:** 15 inches
Light:	Sun to light shade **Soil:** Rich, well-drained; likes lime
Care:	Deadhead for appearance
Uses:	Rock garden, border, edging
Propagation:	Self-sows; does not transplant easily
Problems:	Short-lived and must have good drainage; does not do well in high humidity
Insider's tips:	If you have the proper rock garden site, pasqueflower is a "collector's" plant, with its unusual and ornamental silvery hairs. Other flower colors available are purple, lilac, and white.
Combines with:	*Phlox subulata, Narcissus cyclamineus* 'February Gold', *Viola labradorica, Euphorbia epithymoides* 'Polychroma'

Anemone blanda
GREEK ANEMONE, WINDFLOWER

Plant type:	Bulb **Zone:** 4–8
Flower:	Small, daisylike white, pink, or blue flowers
Foliage:	Small, lacy
Bloom length:	4 weeks
Height:	4–6 inches **Width/spacing:** 6 inches
Light:	Open shade **Soil:** Rich, moist, well-drained
Care:	Winter protection in Zone 4
Uses:	Naturalizes, woodland, gardening in small spaces, early spring color, daisy garden
Propagation:	Divide clumps after bloom; self-sows
Problems:	Summer dormancy; take care when dormant to not dig up
Insider's tips:	This is the easiest of the bulbs because no cutting down is necessary—spent foliage just disappears!
Combines with:	*Narcissus cyclamineus* 'February Gold', *Vinca minor* 'Bowles Variety', *Asarum europaeum*, *Asarum canadense*, *Tulipa greigii* 'Toronto'

Anemonella thalictroides
RUE ANEMONE

Plant type:	Perennial, native, herb **Zone:** 4–8
Flower:	Small, 1-inch white anemone or poppylike shape
Foliage:	Delicate, *Thalictrum*-like, gray-green; emerging foliage is tinged purple.
Bloom length:	4–8 weeks
Height:	8 inches **Width/spacing:** 10 inches
Light:	Part shade, shade **Soil:** Rich, moist, well-drained
Care:	Deadhead if you do not want seeding; shearing the plant may result in repeat bloom
Uses:	Woodland, naturalistic, naturalizes, native, white garden, long bloomer
Propagation:	Division after blooming; self-sows
Problems:	Is not ephemeral, but can go dormant if excessively dry.
Insider's tips:	If allowed to naturalize, rue anemone creates a tapestry on the woodland floor with other diminutive natives.
Combines with:	*Anemone sylvestris, Scilla sibirica, Narcissus cyclamineus* 'February Gold', *Trillium grandiflorum, Phlox divaricata, Stylophorum diphyllum*

Arabis caucasica 'Snowcap'
WALL ROCK CRESS

Plant type:	Perennial, evergreen **Zone:** 4–7
Flower:	White, phloxlike clusters; fragrant
Foliage:	Ever-gray-green; mat-forming
Bloom length:	7–8 weeks
Height:	6–8 inches **Width/spacing:** 12–18 inches
Light:	Full sun to light shade **Soil:** Average, well-drained
Care:	Cut back after blooming to keep compact
Uses:	Rock garden, edging, stone wall, foliage color, fragrance, ground-cover, evergreen
Propagation:	Easiest by stem cuttings in early summer
Problems:	May rot in excessively wet soils
Insider's tips:	One of the few perennials that stay evergreen in the North—or ever-gray-green. Rock garden enthusiasts should also try *Arabis alpina* 'Compinkie' and *Aubrieta deltoidea* 'Purple Gem'.
Combines with:	*Tulipa greigii* 'Toronto', *Phlox stolonifera*, *Heuchera* 'Plum Pudding', *Iris tectorum*

Asarum canadense
CANADIAN WILD GINGER

Plant type:	Perennial, native, groundcover **Zone:** 3–9
Flower:	Juglike, brown, hidden under foliage
Foliage:	Heart-shaped leaves, clump-forming, fuzzy, deciduous
Bloom length:	2–3 weeks
Height:	6–12 inches **Width/spacing:** 12 inches
Light:	Part shade, shade **Soil:** Rich, moist, well-drained
Care:	Easy; hardier and faster-spreading than European ginger
Uses:	Groundcover, shady edger, woodland, naturalistic garden
Propagation:	Division of rhizome in spring
Problems:	None
Insider's tips:	Most people aren't even aware that wild ginger has a bloom because it is so well hidden under the foliage. Canadian ginger spreads to cover ground better than the European ginger.
Combines with:	*Hosta* 'Antioch', *Tiarella wherryi, Adiantum pedatum, Polemonium reptans, Actaea rubra, Dicentra* x 'Luxuriant', *Corydalis lutea*

Bergenia cordifolia
BERGENIA, PIGSQUEAK

Plant type:	Perennial, evergreen **Zone:** 3–9
Flower:	Clusters of rose pink waxy bells on erect, fleshy stems
Foliage:	Evergreen, shiny, cabbage-shaped leaves in rosettes, red fall color
Bloom length:	4–8 weeks
Height:	12 inches **Width/spacing:** 12–18 inches
Light:	Part shade **Soil:** Average, well-drained
Care:	Cut away any foliage that becomes tattered
Uses:	Edger, woodland edge, stream banks, foliage effect
Propagation:	Spreads by rhizomes; divide in spring
Problems:	Control slugs!
Insider's tips:	Made popular by Gertrude Jekyll and often used in sunnier sites in England, *Bergenia* looks best for winter interest in Zones 6 through 9.
Combines with:	*Dicentra* x 'Luxuriant', *Aquilegia alpina*, *Myosotis sylvatica*, *Galium odoratum*

Caltha palustris
MARSH MARIGOLD, COWSLIP

Plant type:	Perennial, native **Zone:** 2–8
Flower:	Yellow-gold, five-petaled buttercup in open clusters
Foliage:	Rounded to heart-shaped, glossy, dark-green mounds
Bloom length:	3 weeks
Height:	12 inches **Width/spacing:** 18 inches
Light:	Sun to light shade
Soil:	Rich, moist—can even grow in standing water
Care:	Do not allow to completely dry out!
Uses:	Bog garden, water's edge, wildflower
Propagation:	Division in summer
Problems:	Must have moisture; summer dormancy
Insider's tips:	This is a great native plant for wet sites. Remember that it will be dormant by summer.
Combines with:	*Primula japonica, Astilbe* cultivars, *Athyrium filix-femina, Osmunda regalis, Iris pseudacorus*

Epimedium 'Crimson'
BISHOP'S HAT

Plant type:	Perennial **Zone:** 5–8
Flower:	Light pink, tiny clusters of "bishop's hats" on wiry stems
Foliage:	Evergreen in some zones; neat mounds of small heart-shaped leaves
Bloom length:	2–4 weeks, depending on temperatures
Height:	8–10 inches **Width/spacing:** 12 inches
Light:	Part shade **Soil:** Rich, moist, well-drained, somewhat acidic
Care:	Likes lots of organic matter, mulch
Uses:	Groundcover, border, edger, rock garden, erosion control
Propagation:	Divide in late summer
Problems:	Cut back browned foliage in early spring
Insider's tips:	*Epimedium* species are becoming collector's plants—just ask popular lecturer and author Cole Burrell! I like to choose those that hold their flowers well above the foliage.
Combines with:	*Carex elata* 'Bowles Golden', *Phlox* x 'Chattahoochee', *Alchemilla mollis, Amsonia tabernaemontana*

Epimedium x *versicolor* 'Sulphureum'
BISHOP'S HAT, BARRENWORT

Plant type:	Perennial, semi-evergreen, groundcover **Zone:** 5–8
Flower:	Yellow, sprays of dainty "bishop's hats"
Foliage:	Compact mound, heart-shaped leaflets, tinted bronze when new
Bloom length:	5 weeks
Height:	12 inches **Width/spacing:** 12 inches
Light:	Part shade, shade **Soil:** Rich, moist, well-drained
Care:	Easy; can even tolerate dry soil
Uses:	Groundcover, shade garden, delicate texture
Propagation:	Division late summer; spread by creeping rhizomes
Problems:	None
Insider's tips:	This is the easiest of the bishop's hats to grow!
Combines with:	*Narcissus* 'Pipit', *Polygonatum commutatum*, *Dicentra spectabilis* 'Alba', *Cimicifuga ramosa* 'Atropurpurea'

Euphorbia epithymoides 'Polychroma'
CUSHION SPURGE

Plant type:	Perennial **Zone:** 3–8
Flower:	Chartreuse yellow bracts
Foliage:	Mound of light green turning mahogany in fall
Bloom length:	3–4 weeks
Height:	12–18 inches **Width/spacing:** 18 inches
Light:	Sun to light shade **Soil:** Average, well-drained
Care:	Shear after blooming to maintain "roundy-moundy" habit
Uses:	Border, edger, rock garden, cottage garden, a blender plant, fall color
Propagation:	Divide in spring
Problems:	Sap may cause skin irritation.
Insider's tips:	The flower color really perks up the spring garden! Chartreuse flowers are very in!
Combines with:	*Tulipa greigii* 'Toronto', *Narcissus* 'Actaea', *Iris tectorum, Iris sibirica* 'Caesar's Brother', *Heuchera* 'Plum Pudding'

Hepatica acutiloba
HEPATICA, LIVERLEAF

Plant type: Perennial, native   **Zone:** 3–7

Flower: Light pink to white, anemone-like

Foliage: Three-lobed, purple-mottled

Bloom length: 1–2 weeks

Height: 4–6 inches   **Width/spacing:** 6 inches

Light: Open shade, needs spring sun to bloom

Soil: Rich, moist, slightly acidic

Care: Do not allow to dry out during the summer.

Uses: Woodland garden, wildflower garden, edger, foliage effect

Propagation: Very slow, by division and by seed

Problems: Will be easily overrun by more vigorous plants

Insider's tips: People who garden in shade treasure these diminutive natives; others wonder what all the fuss is about. It is best to choose other delicate perennials as neighbors so they are not crowded out.

Combines with: *Adiantum pedatum, Tiarella wherryi, Asarum canadense, Myosotis sylvatica, Dicentra cucullaria*

Jeffersonia diphylla
TWINLEAF

Plant type:	Perennial, native **Zone:** 4–8
Flower:	White, eight-petaled, poppylike
Foliage:	Paired leaflets look like green butterflies, hence the name twinleaf
Bloom length:	2–3 weeks
Height:	12–18 inches **Width/spacing:** 12 inches
Light:	Part shade, shade **Soil:** Rich, moist, alkaline
Care:	Easy
Uses:	Woodland, naturalizes, foliage tapestry
Propagation:	Division in fall; self-sows
Problems:	Short bloom time
Insider's tips:	The twin leaves make an interesting foliage tapestry throughout the growing season.
Combines with:	*Anemonella thalictroides, Polystichum acrostichoides, Phlox divaricata, Thalictrum aquilegiifolium, Polygonatum odoratum* 'Variegatum'

Leucojum aestivum 'Gravetye Giant'
SUMMER SNOWFLAKE

Plant type: Bulb **Zone:** 4–7

Flower: Up to eight hanging white bells tipped green

Foliage: Clumps of 12-inch narrow, straplike leaves

Bloom length: 4–5 weeks

Height: 24 inches **Width/spacing:** 24–30 inches

Light: Light shade to full sun **Soil:** Rich, moist, well-drained

Care: Allow foliage to go dormant and feed next season's bulb before removing

Uses: Woodland edge, white garden, cottage garden

Propagation: Divide well-established clumps in five years in late summer

Problems: Does not like roots disturbed; summer dormancy

Insider's tips: Interplant with foliage plants that can disguise fading foliage! 'Gravetye Giant' has larger flowers than the species.

Combines with: *Dryopteris marginalis, Brunnera macrophylla, Stylophorum diphyllum, Dicentra spectabilis, Hosta* 'Antioch'

Mertensia virginica
VIRGINIA BLUEBELLS

Plant type:	Perennial, native **Zone:** 3–8
Flower:	Sky blue, sprays of small nodding bells
Foliage:	Light green ovals along 2-foot stems; emerges purple-tinged
Bloom length:	3 weeks
Height:	24 inches **Width/spacing:** 18 inches
Light:	Part shade—needs sun during bloom, shade tolerant when dormant
Soil:	Rich, moist
Care:	Remove dead foliage when dormant
Uses:	Naturalizes, woodland edge, blooms with spring bulbs, shade garden
Propagation:	Reseeds in moist conditions
Problems:	Summer dormancy
Insider's tips:	Use with plants that will cover dormant plant space. I recommend hostas or groundcovers.
Combines with:	*Hosta* 'Piedmont Gold', *Pachysandra terminalis, Dicentra spectabilis, Stylophorum diphyllum, Narcissus* cultivars

Muscari armeniacum
GRAPE HYACINTH

Plant type:	Bulb **Zone:** 3–8
Flower:	Purple-blue, looks like a cluster of grapes; scented
Foliage:	Grasslike
Bloom length:	4 weeks
Height:	6 inches **Width/spacing:** 6 inches
Light:	Sun to part shade **Soil:** Rich, moist, well-drained
Care:	Easy
Uses:	Naturalizes, rock garden, edging
Propagation:	Divide offsets (I rarely remember to do this.)
Problems:	Summer dormancy
Insider's tips:	Foliage comes up again in fall and can be used as a marker for other bulbs planted. See "Interplanting Bulbs in the Perennial Garden" in chapter 9.
Combines with:	*Narcissus* 'Jack Snipe', *Tulipa* 'Red Emperor', *Arabis caucasica* 'Snowcap', *Anemonella thalictroides, Pulmonaria saccharata* 'Sissinghurst White'

Narcissus cyclamineus 'February Gold'
FEBRUARY GOLD DAFFODIL

Plant type:	Bulb **Zone:** 3–8
Flower:	Small yellow, collared trumpets
Foliage:	Straplike
Bloom length:	2–6 weeks
Height:	6–8 inches **Width/spacing:** 8–10 inches
Light:	Sun to part shade **Soil:** Average, well-drained
Care:	Allow foliage to "feed" the bulb before cutting down
Uses:	Naturalizes, mass in shrub border, interplant with perennials
Propagation:	Divide when foliage turns brown; multiplies rapidly
Problems:	Summer dormancy
Insider's tips:	My clients like this early bloomer because the foliage "ripens" earlier. Foliage can be cut down about six weeks after plant started to bloom—the trick is to mark that date on your calendar!
Combines with:	*Muscari armeniacum, Arabis caucasica* 'Snowcap', *Pulmonaria longifolia* var. *cevennensis, Mertensia virginica, Dicentra* x 'Luxuriant'

Polemonium reptans
CREEPING JACOB'S LADDER

Plant type:	Perennial, native **Zone:** 2–7
Flower:	Light blue; many small bells per stem
Foliage:	Mounded, fernlike leaves arranged to form a ladder
Bloom length:	3–4 weeks
Height:	8–10 inches **Width/spacing:** 12 inches
Light:	Part shade **Soil:** Rich, moist
Care:	Deadhead to maintain moundlike feature; keep moist
Uses:	Woodland edge, border, adds texture, early bloom, naturalizes
Propagation:	Division in late summer; self-sows
Problems:	Dwindles in very shaded sites
Insider's tips:	The mounded, fernlike foliage persists throughout the growing season, adding texture to the shade garden.
Combines with:	*Primula veris, Trillium grandiflorum, Aquilegia canadensis, Asarum canadense, Stylophorum diphyllum, Polygonatum odoratum* 'Variegatum', *Hosta* 'Golden Tiara'

Primula veris
COWSLIP PRIMROSE

Plant type:	Perennial **Zone:** 5–8
Flower:	Fragrant, nodding, clusters of yellow, tubular blooms
Foliage:	Basal rosette of wrinkled ovals
Bloom length:	3–4 weeks
Height:	8 inches **Width/spacing:** 12 inches
Light:	Light shade to part shade
Soil:	Average, well-drained, alkaline soils
Care:	Deadhead for neatness
Uses:	Cottage garden, wildflower, meadow, woodland edge, shade garden, early blooming
Propagation:	Seed
Problems:	Has some difficulty with drying heat
Insider's tips:	This primrose prefers alkaline soils; this means you can grow them in well-drained, amended clay.
Combines with:	*Polemonium reptans, Stylophorum diphyllum, Phlox divaricata, Iris cristata*

Pulmonaria longifolia ssp. *cevennensis*
CEVENNES LUNGWORT

Plant type:	Perennial **Zone:** 3–8
Flower:	Violet-blue clusters of nodding blooms
Foliage:	Long, narrow, hairy leaves with silvery blotches in dense mounds
Bloom length:	7 weeks
Height:	12 inches **Width/spacing:** 15 inches
Light:	Part shade, shade **Soil:** Rich, moist, well-drained
Care:	Keep soil evenly moist; cut back diseased foliage for plant regeneration
Uses:	Woodland, shade garden, wildflower, foliage effect, early blooming
Propagation:	Rarely needs division; self-sows but may not be true to form
Problems:	Slugs, rot and sometimes powdery mildew
Insider's tips:	Most lungworts bloom so early that the foliage is still very juvenile. About a month after bloom, the leaves mature into very showy mounds. 'Bertram Anderson' in another good longifolia selection.
Combines with:	*Helleborus orientalis, Anemonella thalictroides, Anemone sylvestris,* astilbes, hostas, ferns

Stylophorum diphyllum
WOOD POPPY, CELANDINE POPPY

Plant type:	Perennial, native **Zone:** 4–9
Flower:	Large, bright yellow, four-petaled, poppylike; interesting green seed capsule
Foliage:	Heavily scalloped, gray-green
Bloom length:	3–4 weeks; sometimes reblooms
Height:	18 inches **Width/spacing:** 12 inches
Light:	Part shade **Soil:** Rich, moist, well-drained
Care:	Easy
Uses:	Bright color in shade garden, woodland, shady border, naturalizes
Propagation:	Self-sows throughout the garden
Problems:	Self-sowing may be a problem; unwanted seedlings can easily be rogued out.
Insider's tips:	Do not confuse with lesser celandine, *Ranunculus ficaria*, which seeds itself everywhere!
Combines with:	*Mertensia virginica, Leucojum aestivum, Phlox divaricata, Dicentra spectabilis, Iris cristata, Brunnera macrophylla, Polemonium reptans, Dryopteris marginalis, Galium odoratum*

Trillium grandiflorum
TRILLIUM, WAKE ROBIN

Plant type: Perennial, native **Zone:** 3–7

Flower: White, distinctly pointed, three-petaled

Foliage: Three-leaved; may go dormant after bloom

Bloom length: 2–3 weeks

Height: 12–15 inches **Width/spacing:** 12 inches

Light: Shade **Soil:** Rich, moist, well-drained

Care: Avoid any soil compaction

Uses: Wildflower, woodland, early bloom, foliage effect, mass for best effect

Propagation: Division of offsets; seed is very slow

Problems: Deer-browse; deer in Illinois are destroying native colonies of trillium. Do not walk on rhizomes.

Insider's tips: All the native trilliums are worth collecting. This one is the easiest and showiest to grow.

Combines with: *Anemonella thalictroides, Phlox divaricata, Dryopteris marginalis, Polystichum acrostichoides, Stylophorum diphyllum, Mertensia virginica,* other trilliums

Tulipa greigii 'Toronto'
TORONTO TULIP

Plant type:	Bulb **Zone:** 3–7
Flower:	Multiflowering; tangerine red
Foliage:	Blue-gray, almost succulent, sometimes purple-mottled
Bloom length:	4–6 weeks
Height:	12 inches **Width/spacing:** 6 inches
Light:	Sun to light shade **Soil:** Average, well-drained
Care:	Deadhead for neatness
Uses:	Naturalizes, border, mass planting
Propagation:	Buy new bulbs
Problems:	Deer- and rabbit-browse; is short-lived
Insider's tips:	By planting tulip bulbs 8 inches deep, they should be longer-lived.
Combines with:	*Pachysandra terminalis, Anemone blanda, Muscari armeniacum, Vinca minor, Leucojum aestivum, Mertensia virginica, Myosotis sylvatica*

Arisaema triphyllum
JACK-IN-THE-PULPIT

Plant type:	Perennial, native **Zone:** 3–9
Flower:	Purple and green-striped, upward-facing cup with hood, under which is "Jack"; red berries in September
Foliage:	Pairs of three-lobed leaves
Bloom length:	6-plus weeks
Height:	12–18 inches **Width/spacing:** 12 inches
Light:	Shade, part shade **Soil:** Rich, moist
Care:	Plants go dormant early without adequate moisture.
Uses:	Woodland, naturalistic, unusual architectural accent, wet garden
Propagation:	Seeds itself slowly over time
Problems:	Rust—get rid of affected plants as soon as noticed
Insider's tips:	Children of all ages delight in this plant! It grows well with any of the woodland natives, particularly those that grow like groundcovers.
Combines with:	*Asarum canadense, Tiarella wherryi, Anemonella thalictroides, Myosotis sylvatica*

Brunnera macrophylla
SIBERIAN BUGLOSS

Plant type:	Perennial, groundcover **Zone:** 3–8
Flower:	Light bright blue; resembles forget-me-not but has taller looser sprays of flowers
Foliage:	Heart-shaped, rough, dark green leaves; mounded
Bloom length:	3–4 weeks
Height:	12–18 inches **Width/spacing:** 18–24 inches
Light:	Part shade, shade **Soil:** Rich, moist, well-drained
Care:	Deadhead for neatness
Uses:	Naturalizes, shade border, groundcover, open woods
Propagation:	Divide in fall, root cuttings in summer
Problems:	Not drought-tolerant
Insider's tips:	Plants can go dormant in persistent drought. *Brunnera macrophylla* 'Hadspen Cream' has cream variegation on leaf margins but is not as vigorous.
Combines with:	*Epimedium* x *versicolor* 'Sulphureum', *Stylophorum diphyllum*, *Smilacina racemosa, Dicentra spectabilis, Dryopteris marginalis*, astilbes

Dicentra spectabilis
BLEEDING HEART

Plant type: Perennial   **Zone:** 2–9

Flower: Pink, pendulous hearts on arching stems

Foliage: Peony-like; goes dormant in late summer

Bloom length: 10 weeks

Height: 30 inches   **Width/spacing:** 3 feet

Light: Part shade to sun   **Soil:** Rich, moist, well-drained

Care: Cut back when dormant

Uses: Shade border, woodland, wildflower, cottage garden

Propagation: Divide when dormant

Problems: Plan for summer dormancy

Insider's tips: Be sure to plant this behind foliage that will hide its summer dormancy. Dormancy is delayed with adequate moisture during dry spells. The white-flowered cultivar is 'Alba'.

Combines with: *Brunnera macrophylla, Leucojum aestivum* 'Gravetye Giant', *Narcissus, Phlox divaricata, Myosotis sylvatica*

Iberis sempervirens 'Purity'
CANDYTUFT

Plant type: Perennial, evergreen   **Zone:** 4–9

Flower: Bright white, forming pompom clusters

Foliage: Evergreen, needlelike

Bloom length: 4–6 weeks

Height: 8 inches   **Width/spacing:** 12 inches

Light: Sun to light shade   **Soil:** Average, well-drained

Care: Shear after blooming for compactness

Uses: Edging, border, winter interest, rock garden, cottage garden

Propagation: Cuttings taken after blooming

Problems: Sometimes dies out in the North (probably due to wet clay soils)

Insider's tips: Choose any of the cultivars for their short, neat habit. There are some candytufts, such as 'Autumn Snow', that rebloom in the fall.

Combines with: *Paeonia officinalis* 'Flame', *Tulipa greigii* 'Toronto', *Euphorbia epithymoides* 'Polychroma', *Euphorbia myrsinites, Heuchera* 'Plum Pudding'

Phlox x 'Chattahoochee'
CHATTAHOOCHEE WOODLAND PHLOX

Plant type:	Perennial **Zone:** 5–9
Flower:	Pale lavender-blue flowers with ruby eye in loose clusters
Foliage:	Small, shiny leaves forming mounds
Bloom length:	6–7 weeks
Height:	12 inches **Width/spacing:** 18 inches
Light:	Light shade **Soil:** Rich, moist, well-drained
Care:	Shear after blooming for compactness
Uses:	Woodland edge, front of border, shade garden, cottage garden
Propagation:	Division after blooming
Problems:	Short-lived
Insider's tips:	I can't reliably get this plant to come back! But Allan Armitage suggests it flowers itself to death.
Combines with:	*Polygonatum odoratum* 'Variegatum', x *Heucherella alba* 'Bridget Bloom', *Heuchera* 'Plum Pudding', *Salvia* x *superba* 'May Night'

Phlox divaricata
WOODLAND PHLOX

Plant type:	Perennial, native **Zone:** 3–9
Flower:	Fragrant, blue, clusters of five notched petals
Foliage:	Small, dark green; creeper
Bloom length:	8 weeks
Height:	15 inches **Width/spacing:** 18 inches
Light:	Part shade to full sun **Soil:** Rich, moist, well-drained
Care:	Easy
Uses:	Border, woodland edge, edger, fragrance, groundcover, wildflower, cottage garden
Propagation:	Divide after blooming; self-sows
Problems:	Goes dormant in drought
Insider's tips:	I do not deadhead, preferring to let this plant to naturalize by self-sowing.
Combines with:	*Dicentra spectabilis, Trillium grandiflorum, Stylophorum diphyllum, Dodecatheon meadia, Primula veris*

Phlox stolonifera
CREEPING PHLOX

Plant type: Perennial, native, semi-evergreen **Zone:** 2–8

Flower: Lavender to pink clusters of star-shaped flowers

Foliage: Creeping mats of small rounded leaves; semi-evergreen

Bloom length: 6 weeks

Height: 8–10 inches **Width/spacing:** 12 inches

Light: Part shade, shade **Soil:** Rich, moist, well-drained

Care: For neatness, cut back to basal foliage after blooming

Uses: Rock garden, edger, naturalizes, woodland edge, groundcover

Propagation: Division after flowering; stem cuttings

Problems: Not as vigorous a grower as *Phlox divaricata* and does not do well with competition

Insider's tips: The Perennial Plant Association chose *Phlox stolonifera* as the first Perennial Plant of the Year in 1990.

Combines with: *Aquilegia alpina, Anemone sylvestris, Tiarella wherryi, Iris sibirica* 'Caesar's Brother', *Galium odoratum*

Tiarella wherryi
FOAMFLOWER

Plant type:	Perennial, native, semi-evergreen **Zone:** 3–8
Flower:	Clusters of white, tiny, star-shaped flowers; clusters form a spike
Foliage:	Clump-forming, lime green, maplelike leaves; evergreen to semi-evergreen
Bloom length:	6–8 weeks
Height:	12 inches **Width/spacing:** 18 inches
Light:	Part shade, shade **Soil:** Rich, moist, somewhat acidic
Care:	Deadhead for neatness and occasional repeat bloom
Uses:	Shade border, woodland, rock garden, groundcover
Propagation:	Division in spring
Problems:	Watch for frost heaving
Insider's tips:	This species is a nonspreading form of foamflower. Recent breeding programs have resulted in many new cultivars well worth trying.
Combines with:	*Polemonium reptans, Adiantum pedatum, Trillium grandiflorum, Dicentra spectabilis, Asarum europaeum, Corydalis lutea*

Dicentra x 'Luxuriant'
LUXURIANT FRINGED BLEEDING HEART

Plant type:	Perennial **Zone:** 3–9
Flower:	Pink, pendulous heart
Foliage:	Blue-gray, fernlike texture
Bloom length:	17 weeks
Height:	12 inches **Width/spacing:** 18 inches
Light:	Part shade, sun **Soil:** Rich, moist, well-drained
Care:	Deadhead for neatness and repeat bloom
Uses:	Wildflower, woodland edge, shade border, long-blooming
Propagation:	Self-sows; divide in spring
Problems:	Susceptible to crown rot—make sure soils are well drained
Insider's tips:	For white blooms from May to September, try *Dicentra formosa* 'Langtrees'.
Combines with:	*Anemone blanda, Brunnera macrophylla, Asarum europaeum, Asarum canadense, Tiarella wherryi*

CHAPTER 3

May

*The Merry Month
As the Profusion of
Flowers Grows*

Iris cristata
CRESTED IRIS

Plant type:	Perennial, native **Zone:** 3–9
Flower:	Sky blue to violet with golden crest
Foliage:	Lime green, dainty swordlike leaf
Bloom length:	2 weeks
Height:	6 inches **Width/spacing:** 8 inches
Light:	Light to part shade **Soil:** Rich, moist, slightly acidic, sandy
Care:	Take care to not pull up
Uses:	Border edger, woodland, rock garden, naturalizes, wildflower
Propagation:	Division after bloom
Problems:	Very shallow rooted
Insider's tips:	Gardeners in the Midwest do not have much luck with this iris, perhaps because of the need for slight acidity. Paying attention to soil improvement really helps.
Combines with:	*Epimedium* 'Crimson', *Tiarella wherryi, Anemonella thalictroides, Aruncus aethusifolius, Galium odoratum*

Alchemilla mollis
LADY'S MANTLE

Plant type:	Perennial **Zone:** 4–7
Flower:	Yellow-green bracts in frothy sprays
Foliage:	Velvety, gray-green, scalloped leaves resembling a lady's mantle
Bloom length:	4 weeks
Height:	12 inches **Width/spacing:** 24 inches
Light:	Part shade to sun, but not hot afternoon sun
Soil:	Rich, moist, well-drained
Care:	Deadhead for neatness and prolonged bloom; mulch to keep soil moist
Uses:	Front of border, woodland edge, edger, rock garden, cut flower, dried flower
Propagation:	Self-sows
Problems:	Dwindles in too much shade
Insider's tips:	There are several interesting dwarf varieties, like *Alchemilla pubescens* and *Alchemilla alpina*.
Combines with:	*Digitalis purpurea, Iris sibirica* 'Caesar's Brother', *Salvia* x *superba* 'May Night', *Nepeta mussinii* 'Blue Wonder', *Paeonia officinalis* 'Flame', *Rosa* 'Knock Out'

Amsonia tabernaemontana
BLUE STAR

Plant type: Perennial, native   **Zone:** 3–9

Flower: Clusters of pale blue, star-shaped flowers

Foliage: Willowlike foliage on many shrubby stems, turning golden in autumn

Bloom length: 3–4 weeks

Height: 30–36 inches   **Width/spacing:** 24 inches

Light: Part shade to sun   **Soil:** Average to rich, evenly moist

Care: Easy; disease-free; can be cut to 10 inches after bloom for compactness

Uses: Background, trouble-free, cut flower, fall color, blue garden

Propagation: Division early spring or fall

Problems: Sometimes chlorotic in alkaline clay soils

Insider's tips: The golden-yellow fall color is an added attraction of this American native. *Amsonia hubrectii* has the best fall color with finer-textured foliage.

Combines with: *Iris ensata, Digitalis purpurea* 'Alba', *Arisaema triphyllum, Anemone sylvestris, Campanula glomerata* 'Superba', *Geranium* x *magnificum*

Anemone sylvestris
SNOWDROP ANEMONE

Plant type:	Perennial, groundcover **Zone:** 3–7
Flower:	Fragrant, white, cupped, poppylike
Foliage:	Mounded, delicately cut, light green leaves
Bloom length:	7 weeks, plus 1 week in fall
Height:	18 inches **Width/spacing:** 12 inches
Light:	Part shade; tolerates some sun—prefers morning sun
Soil:	Rich, moist, well-drained
Care:	Deadhead for light rebloom in fall
Uses:	Woodland edge, wildflower garden, shade garden, naturalizes, groundcover
Propagation:	Division in fall; root cuttings
Problems:	Runs in loose soils but is easily pulled back
Insider's tips:	Unlike other spring-blooming anemones, it does not go dormant! Dig out excess plants to pass along to friends.
Combines with:	*Anemonella thalictroides, Muscari armeniacum, Dicentra spectabilis, Aquilegia alpina, Amsonia tabernaemontana, Iris sibirica, Corydalis lutea*

Aquilegia alpina
ALPINE COLUMBINE

Plant type:	Perennial **Zone:** 3–8
Flower:	Blue spurs with short curves; slightly nodding
Foliage:	Blue-green, mounded
Bloom length:	6 weeks **Height:** 24–30 inches **Width/spacing:** 12–18 inches
Light:	Sun to part shade; prefers morning sun
Soil:	Light, average, well-drained
Care:	Use insecticidal soap at first sign of leafminer; remove and destroy infected leaves
Uses:	Wildflower garden, attracts hummingbirds, woodland edge, shade garden, cottage garden, cut flower
Propagation:	Self-sows; taproot is sometimes difficult to divide
Problems:	Leafminers and crown rot; short-lived—well-drained soils increase chance for longevity
Insider's tips:	*Aquilegia* x 'Hensol Harebell' is longer lived. When my Alpine columbines disappear, I shamelessly buy in new.
Combines with:	*Myosotis sylvatica, Geranium sanguineum* var. *striatum, Iris sibirica* 'Butter and Sugar', *Paeonia officinalis* 'Krinkled White', *Digitalis grandiflora*

Aquilegia canadensis
WILD COLUMBINE

Plant type: Perennial, native **Zone:** 3–8

Flower: Almost-straight spurs are red, petals are yellow; nodding bloom

Foliage: Blue-green, somewhat evergreen in the South

Bloom length: 4–6 weeks

Height: 2–3 feet **Width/spacing:** 12–18 inches

Light: Part shade, shade **Soil:** Average to sandy, well-drained

Care: Deadhead for neatness

Uses: Wildflower garden, attracts hummingbirds, woodland edge, shade garden, cottage garden, naturalistic

Propagation: Self-sows; plants flower in their second year from seed

Problems: Less susceptible to leafminers

Insider's tips: In the wild, I have seen this growing well in shadier sites than most columbines grow. It's fun to see where they will turn up as seedlings in the garden and how many hummingbirds are attracted!

Combines with: *Hosta* 'Golden Scepter', *Brunnera macrophylla, Mertensia virginica, Trillium sessile, Polygonatum commutatum, Smilacina racemosa*

Aquilegia canadensis 'Corbett'
DWARF COLUMBINE

Plant type:	Perennial **Zone:** 3–8
Flower:	Prolific masses of small, creamy-yellow nodding flowers with short spurs
Foliage:	Gray-green, dome-shaped mounds
Bloom length:	6–8 weeks
Height:	10–12 inches **Width/spacing:** 12 inches
Light:	Sun to part shade—prefers morning sun
Soil:	Rich, moist, well-drained
Care:	Deadhead to basal mound after blooming for a neater appearance
Uses:	Edger, cottage garden, wildflower garden, prolific bloom
Propagation:	Self-sows
Problems:	Less prone to leafminers
Insider's tips:	This has a tighter, more clustered form than other *Aquilegia*, with prolific pale, yellow blooms. Use wherever you need a profusely blooming "roundy-moundy."
Combines with:	*Myosotis sylvatica, Iris tectorum, Brunnera macrophylla, Campanula glomerata* 'Superba'

Asarum europaeum
EUROPEAN GINGER

Plant type:	Perennial, evergreen **Zone:** 4–7
Flower:	Juglike, brown, hidden under foliage
Foliage:	Dark, glossy, heart-shaped, clumped, evergreen (only partially so in the North)
Bloom length:	2–3 weeks
Height:	6 inches **Width/spacing:** 12 inches
Light:	Part shade, shade **Soil:** Rich, moist
Care:	Easy
Uses:	Shady edger, woodland, groundcover
Propagation:	Division of rhizomes in spring
Problems:	Does not tolerate high temperatures; slow to spread
Insider's tips:	The glossy foliage adds reflected light in dark places. The Canadian wild ginger is a better groundcover, as it spreads faster.
Combines with:	*Muscari armeniacum, Phlox divaricata, Aruncus aethusifolius, Astilbe* x *arendsii* 'Rheinland', *Dicentra* x 'Luxuriant', *Corydalis lutea, Galium odoratum*

Baptisia australis
BLUE FALSE INDIGO

Plant type:	Perennial, native **Zone:** 3–8
Flower:	Indigo blue, lupinelike spike followed by dark brown pods
Foliage:	Blue-green, multi-stemmed, bush-sized, soft mass
Bloom length:	3–4 weeks
Height:	3–4 feet **Width/spacing:** 3 feet
Light:	Sun to light shade **Soil:** Rich, moist
Care:	Cut back after blooming to encourage a shrublike form
Uses:	Back of the border, hedge, pods used in dried arrangements, meadow/prairie, attracts butterflies
Propagation:	Division is often difficult and should be done in late fall; occasionally self-sows
Problems:	May need staking if not enough sun
Insider's tips:	Also look for native white-flowered forms: *Baptisia lactea* and *Baptisia leucophaea*. This is a good background plant.
Combines with:	*Paeonia officinalis* 'Flame', *Geranium endressii* 'Wargrave Pink', *Alchemilla mollis*, *Iris sibirica* 'Butter and Sugar', *Oenothera fruticosa* ssp. *glauca*

Camassia leichtlinii
CAMASS, WILD HYACINTH

Plant type:	Bulb, native **Zone:** 5–8
Flower:	Violet-blue stars on a poker-shaped spike on tall stems
Foliage:	2-foot-long straplike foliage that goes dormant after bloom
Bloom length:	4 weeks
Height:	36 inches **Width/spacing:** 10 inches
Light:	Sun to light shade **Soil:** Rich, moist
Care:	Cut back spent foliage and flowers
Uses:	Architectural accent, back of the border, naturalistic garden, mixed border
Propagation:	Seed or new bulbs
Problems:	Foliage can look very messy; plant bulbs among plants with foliage that can hide dieback, such as coneflowers and fountain grass.
Insider's tips:	Interplanting this bulb with other perennials in clusters of three to five shows off these blooms to best effect. Remember to plant at a depth three times the height of the bulb.
Combines with:	*Stylophorum diphyllum, Filipendula rubra, Pennisetum alopecuroides, Echinacea purpurea* 'Magnus'

Campanula glomerata 'Superba'
CLUSTERED BELLFLOWER

Plant type:	Perennial **Zone:** 3–8
Flower:	Deep violet, funnel-shaped in tight clusters
Foliage:	Many stems from basal mat of rough, dark green leaves
Bloom length:	4 weeks
Height:	24–30 inches **Width/spacing:** 12–15 inches
Light:	Sun to part shade; needs part shade in the South
Soil:	Rich, moist, well-drained
Care:	Cut flowering stems back after bloom; deadheading does not prolong the bloom
Uses:	Mid-border, cottage garden, bright color accent, cut flower, prolific
Propagation:	Division in spring or fall; divide every three years to maintain vigor
Problems:	Slugs
Insider's tips:	Although blooming for such a short time, the impact of the dark color really pops out and catches the eye.
Combines with:	*Achillea* 'Moonshine', *Alchemilla mollis, Geranium sanguineum* var. *striatum, Paeonia officinalis* 'Flame', *Rosa* 'Carefree Delight'

Cerastium tomentosum
SNOW-IN-SUMMER

Plant type:	Perennial **Zone:** 2–7
Flower:	White masses of tiny star-shaped blooms
Foliage:	Silver-gray, mat-forming, creeper
Bloom length:	7 weeks
Height:	6 inches **Width/spacing:** 12 inches
Light:	Full sun **Soil:** Average to sandy, well-drained
Care:	Cut back hard after blooming to maintain plant strength; do not fertilize
Uses:	Rock garden, dry walls, edger, foliage color
Propagation:	Divide in spring
Problems:	Rots in wet situations; becomes raggedy if not given proper care
Insider's tips:	Although this has nice foliage color and texture, I rarely use it because the upkeep is too time-consuming.
Combines with:	*Tulipa* cultivars, *Euphorbia myrsinites, Iris tectorum, Campanula glomerata* 'Superba'

Clematis hybrids
VIRGIN'S BOWER, CLEMATIS

Plant type:	Perennial, vine **Zone:** 5–8
Flower:	Showy red, pink, purple, blue, or white six-pointed stars; some doubles available
Foliage:	Dark green, glossy leaves—sometimes in clusters of three—on vining stems
Bloom length:	4–6 weeks **Height:** 6–12 feet **Width/spacing:** 24–36 inches
Light:	Sun to light shade
Soil:	Rich, moist, well-drained; likes alkaline soils
Care:	Spring pruning, guide stems by twining onto supports
Uses:	Background, screening, colorful vertical display
Propagation:	Layering
Problems:	Slow-growing; clematis wilt
Insider's tips:	Don't get discouraged if this vine is slow; it takes about three years to fully mature. Try using cup hooks to train vines on wooden structures.
Combines with:	*Hemerocallis* 'Pink Lavender Appeal', *Dictamnus albus* 'Purpureus', *Lysimachia punctata*, *Campanula glomerata* 'Superba', *Paeonia officinalis* 'Flame'

Dictamnus albus 'Purpureus'
PINK GAS PLANT

Plant type:	Perennial **Zone:** 3–7
Flower:	Pink, outward-facing stars forming a spike; fragrant
Foliage:	Many upright stems give a shrubby appearance; lemony fragrance when crushed
Bloom length:	4 weeks
Height:	30 inches **Width/spacing:** 24 inches
Light:	Sun to light shade **Soil:** Average to rich, well-drained
Care:	Avoid wet soil
Uses:	Background, mixed border, cottage garden, herb garden
Propagation:	Deep roots do not transplant well; seed is sown outdoors in late summer.
Problems:	Slow to mature
Insider's tips:	Plants are slow to achieve mature size, but the wait will be worth it! Don't plan on moving this plant once sited.
Combines with:	*Nepeta sibirica, Baptisia australis, Salvia* x *superba* 'May Night', *Iris sibirica* 'Caesar's Brother', *Allium aflatunense* 'Purple Sensation', *Geranium* x *magnificum*

Dodecatheon meadia
SHOOTING STAR

Plant type:	Perennial, native **Zone:** 5–8
Flower:	Rose, pink, or white, nodding, cyclamen-like with "shooting" yellow stamens
Foliage:	Shiny, oblong leaves in mounds; dormant by July
Bloom length:	3–4 weeks
Height:	9–18 inches **Width/spacing:** 12 inches
Light:	Part shade; no afternoon sun **Soil:** Rich, moist, well-drained
Care:	Mulch to retain soil moisture
Uses:	Woodland edge, shade garden, wildflower, prairie/meadow, naturalistic garden
Propagation:	Division in fall when dormant
Problems:	Summer dormancy
Insider's tips:	Planting companions should have foliage that fills in to cover the space left during summer dormancy. I have never remembered to divide this in fall, but with a little patience, shooting star will naturalize.
Combines with:	*Aster* species, *Asarum canadense*, *Sporobolus heterolepsis*, *Brunnera macrophylla*, *Hosta fluctuans* 'Sagae'

Euphorbia dulcis 'Chameleon'
PURPLE SPURGE

Plant type: Perennial   **Zone:** 5–7

Flower: Yellow-green to chartreuse; rounded bract clusters typical of other spurges

Foliage: Mounds of oblong, bronzed-purple leaves

Bloom length: 4 weeks, but remains a dried flower

Height: 12–15 inches   **Width/spacing:** 15 inches

Light: Full sun   **Soil:** Average to rich, evenly moist

Care: Easy

Uses: Foliage color, cottage garden, edger, cut flower

Propagation: Cuttings in mid-summer, seed

Problems: Gets leggy in shaded sites

Insider's tips: This newer selection has become popular because of the wonderful foliage color and the tightly mounded habit. They do best without heat and humidity.

Combines with: *Rosa* 'Showbiz', *Campanula glomerata* 'Superba', *Campanula carpatica* 'Deep Blue Clips', *Iris tectorum*

Euphorbia myrsinites
DONKEYTAIL SPURGE

Plant type:	Perennial, drought-tolerant **Zone:** 5–9
Flower:	Chartreuse clustered bracts
Foliage:	Prostrate fleshy stems with whorls of blue-gray leaves; ever blue-gray
Bloom length:	4–6 weeks
Height:	8 inches, trailing **Width/spacing:** 12–15 inches
Light:	Full sun **Soil:** Average, well-drained
Care:	Winter stems get a bit straggly and should be cut back in late winter; cut back again after blooming to keep tightly mounded
Uses:	Rock garden, edger, cut flower, containers, unusual foliage color and form
Propagation:	Cuttings taken after blooming; self-sows
Problems:	Rots in overly wet soils; milky sap may cause skin irritation
Insider's tips:	Self-sows prolifically if soil is well drained (in everyone else's garden but mine!).
Combines with:	*Myosotis sylvatica* x 'Anthea', *Sedum* x 'Vera Jameson', *Campanula carpatica*, *Callirhoe involucrata*, *Salvia* x *superba* 'May Night'

Galium odoratum
SWEET WOODRUFF

Plant type: Perennial, herb, groundcover   **Zone:** 3–8

Flower: Tiny, white four-pointed star in clusters

Foliage: Star-shaped, fragrant when crushed—like new-mown hay

Bloom length: 3 weeks

Height: 6 inches   **Width/spacing:** 12 inches, spreading

Light: Part shade, shade   **Soil:** Rich, moist, well-drained

Care: If foliage "browns out" in summer, cut back to refoliate.

Uses: Edger , woodland, groundcover, blender and weaver, flavors May wine, fixative in perfume and potpourri

Propagation: Division in spring

Problems: Moderately invasive; pull back unwanted plants

Insider's tips: Like a delicate, miniature *Pachysandra*, sweet woodruff makes a good groundcover but an even better "blender and weaver" of the woodland garden.

Combines with: *Heuchera* 'Plum Pudding', *Myosotis sylvatica*, *Hosta* 'Albo-Marginata', *Polystichum acrostichoides*, *Astilbe* cultivars, *Asarum europaeum*

Geranium x *cantabrigiense* 'Biokovo'
CRANESBILL

Plant type:	Perennial, groundcover **Zone:** 4–8
Flower:	Pink-tinged, white, cup-shaped
Foliage:	Spreading, star-shaped foliage
Bloom length:	4–5 weeks
Height:	12 inches **Width/spacing:** 12 inches, spreading
Light:	Full sun **Soil:** Rich, moist, well-drained
Care:	Deadhead for neatness
Uses:	Groundcover, edger, cottage garden, filler
Propagation:	Division in fall
Problems:	None
Insider's tips:	I do love the perennial geraniums! I try to pick different flower colors and plant habits to use throughout the landscape.
Combines with:	*Iris pumila, Iris pallida* 'Argentea-variegata', *Myosotis sylvatica, Nepeta mussinii* 'Blue Wonder'

Geranium endresii 'Wargrave Pink'
WARGRAVE PINK CRANESBILL

Plant type: Perennial, drought-tolerant   **Zone:** 4–8

Flower: Rich pink, cup-shaped, five-petaled; petals are notched

Foliage: Loose, mounding, star-shaped leaves

Bloom length: 6–8 weeks; some repeat throughout summer

Height: 18 inches   **Width/spacing:** 24 inches

Light: Sun to light shade   **Soil:** Rich, moist, well-drained

Care: Deadhead to encourage repeat bloom; cut back to new growth if the foliage flops

Uses: Cottage garden, border, mid-border, filler

Propagation: Division in fall

Problems: Likely to sprawl after blooming

Insider's tips: Other cultivars, 'Claridge Druce' and 'A. T. Johnson', are said to bloom more prolifically.

Combines with: *Bergenia cordifolia, Iris sibirica* 'Caesar's Brother', *Campanula glomerata* 'Superba', *Helictotrichon sempervirens, Heuchera* 'Plum Pudding'

Geranium maculatum
WILD GERANIUM

Plant type: Perennial, native **Zone:** 4–8

Flower: Rose to mauve, upfacing, five-petaled saucers

Foliage: Mounded, maplelike leaves

Bloom length: 3–5 weeks

Height: 24 inches **Width/spacing:** 18 inches

Light: Light shade to shade **Soil:** Rich, moist, well-drained

Care: Easy

Uses: Woodland, meadow, wildflower garden, cottage garden, shady garden, naturalizes

Propagation: Take side shoots in spring; self-sows

Problems: None

Insider's tips: I have been collecting the very showy, white-flowered *Geranium maculatum* 'Album' for my shade garden. Both flower best with a little bit of sunlight.

Combines with: *Athyrium filix-femina, Dryopteris marginalis, Hosta* 'Halcyon', *Hesperis matronalis, Allium aflatunense* 'Purple Sensation', *Brunnera macrophylla, Phlox divaricata*

Geranium x *magnificum*
GERANIUM, SPANISH CRANESBILL

Plant type: Perennial   **Zone:** 3–8

Flower: Violet-blue, profuse five-petaled flower on loose stems

Foliage: Large, dark green, maplelike leaves in mounds turning purple-red in fall

Bloom length: 5–6 weeks

Height: 24–30 inches   **Width/spacing:** 24 inches

Light: Sun to light shade   **Soil:** Average, well-drained

Care: Cut back entire plant after blooming to regenerate more-compact foliage

Uses: Mid-border, fall color, cut flower, profuse bloom, showy color

Propagation: Division in spring

Problems: Flops in wind and rain—a peony hoop sometimes helps

Insider's tips: If you love blue, this is the geranium for you!

Combines with: *Alchemilla mollis, Buddleia davidii* 'Royal Red', *Phlox maculata* 'Miss Lingard', *Rosa* 'Carefree Delight'

Hesperis matronalis
DAME'S ROCKET

Plant type:	Perennial **Zone:** 3–8
Flower:	Fragrant white, lavender-purple, or mauve phloxlike blooms on spires
Foliage:	Phloxlike with basal rosette; stems rise from a basal clump
Bloom length:	6 weeks
Height:	36 inches **Width/spacing:** 18 inches
Light:	Part shade to sun **Soil:** Average to moist
Care:	Deadheading does result in rebloom; allow some reseeding
Uses:	Border, wildflower, cottage garden, fragrance, naturalizes, back of the border
Propagation:	Self-sows
Problems:	Sometimes becomes floppy
Insider's tips:	Most years this plant acts like a reseeding annual. I have plants that come back each year in the same place as perennials, but I feel gardeners should treat is as a reseeding annual, just in case. Plants are not found in most catalogs; to assure next year's plants, allow some to seed or get seeds from a friend.
Combines with:	*Aquilegia alpina, Alchemilla mollis, Iris germanica, Iris sibirica, Paeonia officinalis* 'Krinkled White', *Allium aflatunense* 'Purple Sensation', *Heuchera* 'Plum Pudding'

Iris pallida 'Argentea-variegata'
VARIEGATED SWEET IRIS

Plant type:	Perennial **Zone:** 3–9
Flower:	Light violet, not a heavy bloomer
Foliage:	Upright, white-variegated, blue-gray blades; effective all season
Bloom length:	2–4weeks
Height:	18 inches **Width/spacing:** 15 inches
Light:	Sun to light shade **Soil:** Rich, moist, well-drained, alkaline
Care:	Keep top of rhizome exposed to the sun
Uses:	Foliage effect, cottage garden, edger, water garden, border
Propagation:	Division after bloom
Problems:	Susceptible to borers and rot, but less so than other irises
Insider's tips:	I prefer the white-variegated form to the creamy-yellow of 'Variegata'. Foliage variegation breaks up an all-green look to the garden and is very showy, even as it emerges.
Combines with:	*Primula japonica, Myosotis sylvatica, Campanula carpatica* 'Deep Blue Clips, *Coreopsis verticillata* 'Moonbeam'

Iris sibirica 'Caesar's Brother'
CAESAR'S BROTHER SIBERIAN IRIS

Plant type: Perennial **Zone:** 3–9

Flower: Purple-blue, consisting of three falls and three standards

Foliage: Clump-forming, upright linear straps

Bloom length: 2–4 weeks

Height: 2–3 feet **Width/spacing:** 18 inches

Light: Sun to part shade **Soil:** Rich, moist

Care: Benefits from a dusting of bonemeal in early spring

Uses: Border, foliage effect, seedpods add interest, trouble-free, cut flower

Propagation: Division after blooming

Problems: Drier soils produce shorter plants

Insider's tips: Although Siberian irises do not have the color range of bearded iris, they are less susceptible to borer and soft rot. Mike Heger (lecturer and owner of Ambergate Gardens in Minnesota) suggests trying those that rebloom, like *Iris sibirica* 'Dancing Nanou'.

Combines with: *Leucanthemum vulgare, Hemerocallis flava, Malva alcea* 'Fastigiata', *Phlox maculata* 'Miss Lingard', *Rosa* 'Carefree Wonder'

Iris tectorum
ROOFTOP IRIS

Plant type:	Perennial **Zone:** 4–8
Flower:	A more open, lavender iris-type flower; two per stem
Foliage:	Chartreuse or yellow-green, relaxed straps; sometimes evergreen
Bloom length:	4–5 weeks
Height:	12–15 inches **Width/spacing:** 18 inches
Light:	Sun to light shade **Soil:** Rich, moist, well-drained
Care:	Deadhead for neatness
Uses:	Edger, foliage effect, herb garden, cottage garden
Propagation:	Division after blooming
Problems:	Disease-prone with too much shade
Insider's tips:	I don't know why rooftop iris is not readily available in the North. I ordered mine from Piccadilly Farm in Bishop, Georgia.
Combines with:	*Coreopsis verticillata* 'Moonbeam', *Geranium sanguineum* var. *striatum, Geranium* x *cantabrigiense* 'Biokovo', *Aster novae-angliae* 'Purple Dome', *Myosotis sylvatica*

Lamium maculatum 'Beedham's White'
BEEDHAM'S WHITE SPOTTED NETTLE

Plant type: Perennial, groundcover **Zone:** 3–8

Flower: White, short spiky cluster

Foliage: Bright yellow-chartreuse leaves with a white stripe down the center; spreading mounds

Bloom length: 8-plus weeks; some fall rebloom

Height: 8 inches **Width/spacing:** 18–24 inches

Light: Part shade, shade; tolerates morning sun

Soil: Average to poor, well-drained

Care: Deadhead for neatness

Uses: Bright accent, woodland edger, groundcover, all-season foliage interest

Propagation: Division anytime; cuttings

Problems: Occasionally slugs

Insider's tips: If planted in masses, it becomes a blanket of gold that really brightens the shade garden!

Combines with: *Helleborus orientalis, Viola labradorica, Polygonatum commutatum, Brunnera macrophylla*

Lamium maculatum 'White Nancy'
WHITE NANCY SPOTTED NETTLE

Plant type:	Perennial, groundcover **Zone:** 3–8
Flower:	White, short spiky cluster
Foliage:	Silvery-white variegation; sometimes evergreen
Bloom length:	8-plus weeks; some fall rebloom
Height:	8 inches **Width/spacing:** 15–24 inches
Light:	Part shade, shade; tolerates morning sun
Soil:	Average to poor, well-drained
Care:	Cut back for compact growth
Uses:	Bright accent, woodland edger, groundcover, all-season foliage interest
Propagation:	Division anytime; stem cuttings
Problems:	May brown out and get straggly; sheer to regenerate new foliage
Insider's tips:	The silvery-white variegation highlights the edge of a shade garden and catches the eye from a good distance.
Combines with:	*Iris sibirica* 'Caesar's Brother', *Aruncus aethusifolius*, *Alchemilla mollis*, *Astilbe* x *arendsii* 'Fanal', *Hosta* 'Halcyon'

Leucanthemum vulgare (syn. *Chrysanthemum leucanthemum*)
OXEYE DAISY, COMMON FIELD DAISY

Plant type:	Perennial **Zone:** 3–9
Flower:	Profuse white daisies with yellow centers
Foliage:	Lanky stems rise from mat-forming basal clusters
Bloom length:	5–6 weeks
Height:	18–24 inches **Width/spacing:** 18 inches, spreading
Light:	Sun to light shade **Soil:** Average to poor, well-drained
Care:	Cut back after blooming
Uses:	Cottage garden, meadow garden, weaver and blender, naturalizes, mid-border, daisy garden
Propagation:	Division anytime
Problems:	Spreads by rhizomes and self-sows—a little bit goes a long way; lanky stems need supporting companion plants.
Insider's tips:	Oxeye daisy bridges the daisy season, as it follows *Anemone blanda* and precedes the Shastas.
Combines with:	*Hemerocallis fulva, Iris sibirica* 'Caesar's Brother', *Alchemilla mollis, Helictotrichon sempervirens*, Asiatic hybrid lilies

Lysimachia nummularia 'Aureus'
GOLDEN MONEYWORT, GOLDEN COINS

Plant type:	Perennial, groundcover **Zone:** 3–9
Flower:	Small, bright-yellow flowers are barely noticeable
Foliage:	Yellow-green, small, round leaves, spreading groundcover
Bloom length:	3 weeks
Height:	6 inches **Width/spacing:** 12 inches, spreading
Light:	Part shade to sun **Soil:** Average to rich, evenly moist
Care:	Shear faded blooms
Uses:	Groundcover, edger, water's edge, shade garden, foliage color
Propagation:	Division in spring and fall; stem cuttings
Problems:	A bit of a spreader, it may need to be pulled back.
Insider's tips:	This moneywort has only sporadic bloom compared to the species also pictured here; it is also less invasive. The foliage brightens dark areas but languishes in dense shade.
Combines with:	*Campanula poscharskyana, Platycodon grandiflorus* 'Sentimental Blue', *Myosotis sylvatica, Aruncus aethusifolius, Hosta* 'Gold Standard'

Lysimachia punctata
WHORLED LOOSESTRIFE, CIRCLE FLOWER

Plant type:	Perennial **Zone:** 4–8
Flower:	Whorls of up-facing golden-yellow bells; each flower center has a circle of brown
Foliage:	Pointed dark-green leaves whorl about the stems, with a similar habit to lilies
Bloom length:	4–6 weeks
Height:	30–36 inches **Width/spacing:** 24-plus inches
Light:	Sun to part shade **Soil:** Rich, moist; tolerates drier sites
Care:	Divide every two years to curb spread
Uses:	Massing, cottage garden, mid-border, wet garden, architectural accent
Propagation:	Division after blooming; stem cuttings
Problems:	Watch for invasiveness—not as invasive as gooseneck loosestrife
Insider's tips:	I have seen this used more often in English gardens than in America, perhaps because we like more "controlled" plant material.
Combines with:	*Campanula glomerata* 'Superba', *Paeonia officinalis* 'Krinkled White', *Geranium* x *magnificum*, *Iris pallida* 'Argentea-variegata', *Iris sibirica* 'Caesar's Brother'

Myosotis sylvatica
FORGET-ME-NOT

Plant type:	Perennial **Zone:** 3–8
Flower:	Tiny, sky-blue with yellow eye
Foliage:	Sprawling, mouse-ear leaves
Bloom length:	4–8 weeks
Height:	6–8 inches **Width/spacing:** 10 inches
Light:	Part shade **Soil:** Rich, moist; does well in considerable moisture
Care:	Cut back for neatness
Uses:	Edger, woodland, naturalizes, weaver and bender
Propagation:	Self-sows prolifically
Problems:	Often shallow-rooted, so it's easily pulled out; prone to powdery mildew in dry soils
Insider's tips:	*Myosotis sylvatica* 'Marina' and 'Royal Blue' have brighter blue flowers with a compact habit. *Myosotis scorpioides* is the forget-me-not for the wet garden.
Combines with:	*Alchemilla mollis, Euphorbia myrsinites, Hosta sieboldiana* 'Elegans', *Hosta* 'Golden Scepter', *Helleborus orientalis, Astilbe* x *arendsii* 'Fanal', *Iris sibirica* 'Butter and Sugar'

Paeonia officinalis 'Flame'
PEONY

Plant type:	Perennial, shrublike **Zone:** 2–8
Flower:	Coral-pink single flower with many frilly yellow stamens
Foliage:	Glossy, leafy, shrublike foliage has a red-purple fall color
Bloom length:	2–4 weeks
Height:	2–3 feet **Width/spacing:** 3–4 feet
Light:	Sun to light shade **Soil:** Rich, moist, well-drained
Care:	Plant eyes (new buds) 2 inches below soil level
Uses:	Cut flower, background foliage, specimen plant, hedge, cottage garden, border
Propagation:	Division in fall (but I never divide peonies)
Problems:	Taller selections of peonies and double flowers need "hooping," but this one does not. The double-flowered peonies can trap rain, leading to diseases such as botrytis.
Insider's tips:	Treat the plant as you would a shrub in design. Another good single-flowered type is *Paeonia* 'Krinkled White'.
Combines with:	*Iris sibirica* 'Caesar's Brother', *Alchemilla mollis*, *Helictotrichon sempervirens*, *Dictamnus albus* 'Purpureus'

Polygonatum commutatum (P. giganteum)
SOLOMON'S SEAL

Plant type:	Perennial, native **Zone:** 5–9
Flower:	Greenish-white, dangling clusters of almost bell-like "seals" along arching stems
Foliage:	Arching stems with paired leaves
Bloom length:	4–6 weeks
Height:	3–7 feet **Width/spacing:** 18 inches, spreading
Light:	Part shade, shade **Soil:** Rich, moist
Care:	Allow to naturalize
Uses:	Woodland, shady border, naturalizes, architectural accent, foliage effect
Propagation:	Divide anytime after blooming; root cuttings
Problems:	With time this may over-colonize; rogue out unwanted plants
Insider's tips:	I love the architectural effect of Solomon's seal with the early spring natives and then later with all the hostas. My Solomon's seals have matured in the three-foot range. So far I have none at seven feet!
Combines with:	*Pulmonaria longifolia* ssp. *cevennensis, Mertensia virginica, Dryopteris marginalis, Brunnera macrophylla, Phlox divaricata, Thalictrum aquilegiifolium, Anemonella thalictroides, Anemone sylvestris*

Polygonatum odoratum 'Variegatum'
VARIEGATED SOLOMON'S SEAL

Plant type:	Perennial **Zone:** 3–9
Flower:	Fragrant, greenish-white, dangling in pairs; black fruit late summer
Foliage:	Alternating oval leaves with white edges on arching stems, yellow fall color
Bloom length:	2–3 weeks
Height:	24 inches **Width/spacing:** 15–18 inches
Light:	Shade, part shade **Soil:** Rich, moist
Care:	Easy
Uses:	Woodland, shady border, naturalizes, architectural accent, foliage effect, fragrance, fall color
Propagation:	Division in fall
Problems:	Slow to form clumps; sawfly larvae may damage leaves
Insider's tips:	The white variegation stands out in the shade garden and is made showier with companions that have white blossoms.
Combines with:	*Myosotis sylvatica, Amsonia tabernaemontana, Thalictrum aquilegiifolium* 'Album', *Trillium grandiflorum, Geranium maculatum* 'Album', *Dryopteris marginalis, Aquilegia canadensis*

Primula japonica
JAPANESE PRIMROSE

Plant type:	Perennial **Zone:** 5–7
Flower:	Red, rose, pink, white, purple-red, crimson, or pink ball-shaped clusters
Foliage:	Basal rosette of rough, paddlelike, crinkled leaves; stems hold blooms in a whorl
Bloom length:	3–4 weeks
Height:	18 inches **Width/spacing:** 12 inches
Light:	Part shade; no afternoon sun **Soil:** Rich, moist, acidic
Care:	Deadheading sometimes results in late-summer bloom
Uses:	Shade garden, water's edge, wildflower, naturalizes
Propagation:	Division in fall
Problems:	Needs a loose soil, has difficulty in clay
Insider's tips:	Although others in the Midwest have had luck with this primrose, I do not seem to have a suitable garden site. Paying close attention to soil preparation should bring success.
Combines with:	*Myosotis sylvatica, Iris pseudacorus, Rodgersia aesculifolia, Astilbe* cultivars, *Caltha palustris*

Saponaria ocymoides 'Max Frei'
MAX FREI ROCK SOAPWORT

Plant type: Perennial   **Zone:** 2–7

Flower: Bright pink, five-petaled in loose sprays

Foliage: Olive green, trailing

Bloom length: 4–5 weeks

Height: 6 inches   **Width/spacing:** 12 inches

Light: Full sun   **Soil:** Average, well-drained

Care: Cut back carefully after flowering for compactness

Uses: Rock garden, walls, edger, slopes

Propagation: Cuttings taken in early summer

Problems: Short-lived

Insider's tips: Avoid the floppy, straggler *Saponaria officianalis* (bouncing bet), which self-sows prolifically!

Combines with: *Iris pumila, Campanula carpatica* 'Deep Blue Clips', *Artemisia stelleriana* 'Silver Brocade', *Geranium* x *cantabrigiense* 'Biokovo'

Smilacina racemosa
SOLOMON'S PLUME, FALSE SOLOMON'S SEAL

Plant type: Perennial, native   **Zone:** 3–7

Flower: White plumes at end of arching stems; fragrant, red fruit

Foliage: Arching stems with zigzagging, lancelike leaves, yellow fall color

Bloom length: 4 weeks

Height: 24–30 inches   **Width/spacing:** 24 inches

Light: Part shade, dappled shade

Soil: Rich, moist; tolerates acidic, sandy soils

Care: Easy

Uses: Woodland, naturalizes, wildflower garden, fruit attracts birds, water's edge, wet garden

Propagation: Division after blooming

Problems: May go dormant during drought

Insider's tips: Underground roots will eventually form dense colonies and can hold soil against erosion. Red berries that form right after blooming are snatched quickly by birds and small animals.

Combines with: *Thalictrum aquilegiifolium, Arisaema triphyllum, Aquilegia canadensis, Dryopteris marginalis, Trillium grandiflorum, Brunnera macrophylla*

Thalictrum aquilegiifolium 'Album'
COLUMBINE MEADOWRUE

Plant type:	Perennial **Zone:** 5–8
Flower:	Panicles of fluffy, white pompoms
Foliage:	Blue-green foliage is small and columbine-like
Bloom length:	2–4 weeks
Height:	36 inches **Width/spacing:** 24 inches
Light:	Part shade **Soil:** Rich, moist
Care:	Easy care; may deadhead into foliage for aesthetics
Uses:	Woodland, naturalistic, wildflower, shaded meadow
Propagation:	Seed sown in early summer is best; division is less reliable.
Problems:	Difficult to find for sale
Insider's tips:	The white flowers really show up in dark situations, and the delicate leaves offset bolder foliage. *Thalictrum aquilegiifolium* 'Roseum' is a nice, light pink improvement over the species.
Combines with:	*Hesperis matronalis, Allium aflatunense* 'Purple Sensation', *Hosta fluctuans* 'Sagae', *Cimicifuga ramosa* 'Atropurpurea', *Arisaema triphyllum*

Trollius chinensis
GLOBEFLOWER

Plant type:	Perennial **Zone:** 3–8
Flower:	Golden orange, globular clusters of petals, showy fringe of stamens in the center
Foliage:	Ornamental, deeply cut, lobed mounds of leaves
Bloom length:	6 weeks; some repeat later in the season
Height:	20 inches **Width/spacing:** 18 inches
Light:	Sun to part shade **Soil:** Rich, moist
Care:	Cut back foliage as it begins to decline in summer
Uses:	Mid-border, cottage garden, unusual form, bright color, wet garden
Propagation:	Division in fall; does not bloom the first year after division
Problems:	Not heat- or drought-tolerant
Insider's tips:	The moisture content of the soil is the key to success with globe-flower. Soil must be constantly moist—even wet.
Combines with:	*Lupinus* (white cultivar), *Myosotis sylvatica*, *Campanula glomerata* 'Superba', *Geranium* x *magnificum*, *Iris sibirica* 'Caesar's Brother'

Uvularia grandiflora
BIG MERRYBELLS

Plant type: Perennial, native   **Zone:** 3–9

Flower: Creamy yellow, hanging bell

Foliage: Bright green, lancelike leaves wrap around upright stems that nod at the tips.

Bloom length: 3–4 weeks

Height: 24–30 inches   **Width/spacing:** 12 inches

Light: Shade, part shade   **Soil:** Rich, moist, well-drained

Care: Easy

Uses: Shade border, woodland, shade garden, wildflower, architectural accent

Propagation: Division in fall; self-sows

Problems: Occasionally slugs

Insider's tips: Shade gardeners use woodland natives for a naturalistic look, as well as for the tapestry of foliage added to the shade garden.

Combines with: *Mertensia virginica, Trillium grandiflorum, Dicentra spectabilis, Phlox divaricata, Anemonella thalictroides*

Viola labradorica
LABRADOR VIOLET

Plant type:	Perennial, native **Zone:** 3–8
Flower:	Purple-violet flowers held above leaves
Foliage:	Purple-tinged mounds of heart-shaped leaves
Bloom length:	4 weeks
Height:	6–8 inches **Width/spacing:** 8 inches
Light:	Part shade, shade **Soil:** Average to rich, evenly moist
Care:	Easy
Uses:	Edger, foliage color, woodland, naturalistic, attracts butterflies
Propagation:	Self-sows; division in late summer
Problems:	None
Insider's tips:	The foliage is the main attraction of this woodland native and is showiest used with plants having light green to chartreuse leaves. At the nursery, choose Labrador violets with the darkest foliage. Another new violet to look for with silvered and swirled foliage is *Viola* 'Dancing Geisha'.
Combines with:	*Lamium maculatum* 'Beedham's White', *Hosta* 'Frances Williams', *Tiarella wherryi, Galium odoratum, Adiantum pedatum*

Aquilegia longissima 'Maxistar'
MAXISTAR LONG-SPURRED COLUMBINE

Plant type:	Perennial **Zone:** 4–9
Flower:	Yellow, long-spurred flower held wandlike above foliage
Foliage:	Gray-green, dome-shaped mounds of scalloped leaves
Bloom length:	10-plus weeks **Height:** 3 feet **Width/spacing:** 18 inches
Light:	Part shade to sun; prefers morning sun
Soil:	Rich, moist, well-drained
Care:	Deadhead for extended bloom; cut back if excessive leafminer damage
Uses:	Mid-border, cottage garden, wildflower garden, long period of bloom, attracts hummingbirds
Propagation:	Buy new plants because it's difficult to divide and self-sown seed is not reliable.
Problems:	Leafminers; short-lived—needs to be replaced in three years
Insider's tips:	This longest-blooming columbine is particularly showy when used against an evergreen background. A cultivar of the Texas native columbine, it tolerates less sun in the South.
Combines with:	*Amsonia tabernaemontana, Iris sibirica* 'Caesar's Brother', *Baptisia australis, Geranium* x *magnificum, Paeonia suffruticosa* (tree peony)

Centaurea montana
PERENNIAL BACHELOR'S BUTTON, MOUNTAIN BLUET

Plant type:	Perennial **Zone:** 3–8
Flower:	Rich blue with a reddish center, fringed
Foliage:	Gray-green, hairy in large cascading mounds of relaxed stems
Bloom length:	6 weeks
Height:	24–30 inches **Width/spacing:** 24 inches
Light:	Sun to part shade **Soil:** Average, well-drained
Care:	Deadhead for repeat bloom and cutback to the basal foliage mound for neatness
Uses:	Cottage garden, wildflower garden, unusual flower form
Propagation:	Spreads by runners and may self-sow; division in spring every three years
Problems:	Floppy; can be aggressive in rich soils
Insider's tips:	This is an incredible blue flower that is hard to pass up, but any gardener must first consider the maintenance involved in keeping the plant looking attractive!
Combines with:	*Helictotrichon sempervirens, Phlox maculata* 'Miss Lingard', *Artemisia ludoviciana* 'Valerie Finnis', *Leucanthemum vulgare, Alchemilla mollis, Geranium* x *cantabrigiense* 'Biokovo'

Dianthus x *allwoodii* 'Doris'
GARDEN PINKS

Plant type: Perennial, evergreen   **Zone:** 4–8

Flower: Pink with darker center, fringed, like a small carnation, fragrant

Foliage: Blue-green, tufted mats, evergreen

Bloom length: 4–6 weeks, and repeat

Height: 9–12 inches   **Width/spacing:** 15 inches

Light: Full sun   **Soil:** Average, well-drained, sandy

Care: Never mulch over shallow roots; deadhead for repeat bloom

Uses: Edger, rock garden, cottage garden, front of the border, herb garden, winter interest, foliage color

Propagation: Cuttings

Problems: Rabbits love to graze; rots in wet soils

Insider's tips: Pinks need well-drained soil! Planting along stone or brick paths laid in sand is ideal.

Combines with: *Coreopsis verticillata* 'Moonbeam', *Campanula carpatica* 'Deep Blue Clips', *Iris pumila*, *Rosa* 'Knock Out'

x *Heucherella alba* 'Bridget Bloom'
FOAMY BELLS

Plant type:	Perennial **Zone:** 3–7
Flower:	A profusion of tiny, pink bells on wiry stems (like *Heuchera*)
Foliage:	Clumps of small maplelike leaves (like *Tiarella*)
Bloom length:	8 weeks
Height:	18 inches **Width/spacing:** 12 inches
Light:	Part shade, will tolerate sun in the morning
Soil:	Rich, moist, well-drained
Care:	Deadhead for repeat bloom
Uses:	Shade garden, woodland edge, edger, long bloomer
Propagation:	Division in fall
Problems:	Rabbits like to nibble; not as vigorous in the South
Insider's tips:	A cross between coral bells and foamflower, 'Bridget Bloom' is impressive for its long bloom time and profusion of flowers. It comes from breeding at Blooms of Bressingham in England.
Combines with:	*Hosta sieboldiana*, *Heuchera* 'Plum Pudding', *Hakonechloa macra* 'Aureola', *Lamium maculatum* 'White Nancy', *Astilbe simplicifolia* 'Praecox Alba'

Stachys byzantina
LAMB'S EARS

Plant type:	Perennial, semi-evergreen **Zone:** 4–7
Flower:	Wooly felted spikes with small, rosy blooms
Foliage:	Silvery-white, felted mats of foliage that resemble lamb's ears
Bloom length:	6 weeks
Height:	12–15 inches **Width/spacing:** 15 inches
Light:	Full sun; afternoon shade in the South
Soil:	Average to poor, well-drained
Care:	Must have well-drained soils; deadhead floppy flowers; deadleaf browned foliage
Uses:	Cottage garden, edger, rock garden, foliage color
Propagation:	Division after blooming
Problems:	Rots with too much water and humidity; flower spikes flop
Insider's tips:	Children love to feel the soft lamb's ear foliage! But this is a high-maintenance plant; try the nonflowering 'Silver Carpet'.
Combines with:	*Digitalis purpurea, Nepeta sibirica, Geranium sanguineum* var. *striatum, Sedum* x 'Autumn Joy'

Stachys officinalis 'Alba'
WOOD BETONY

Plant type:	Perennial, herb **Zone:** 4–8
Flower:	Small white flowers whorl to form a spike
Foliage:	Dark green, scalloped, lancelike leaves form tight clumps
Bloom length:	6–10 weeks
Height:	18–24 inches **Width/spacing:** 18 inches
Light:	Part shade to sun **Soil:** Average, well-drained
Care:	Deadhead for neatness and repeat bloom later in the season
Uses:	Edger, long bloomer, cottage garden, herb garden, cut flower
Propagation:	Division in fall
Problems:	Hard to find in nurseries
Insider's tips:	The betonies are a little-known group of plants that should be used more often in the perennial border. *Stachys monieri* is an outstanding pink-flowered dwarf. See Canyon Creek Nursery in Oroville, California, to order by mail.
Combines with:	*Astilbe japonica* 'Fanal', *Aquilegia longissima* 'Maxistar', *Campanula carpatica* 'Deep Blue Clips', *Viola labradorica*, *Hemerocallis* 'Happy Returns'

Geranium sanguineum var. *striatum* (syn. 'Lancastriense')
BLOODY CRANESBILL, HARDY GERANIUM

Plant type:	Perennial, drought-tolerant **Zone:** 3–8
Flower:	Light pink with darker veining, saucerlike, dainty, free-flowering blooms
Foliage:	Low-growing mounds of star-shaped leaves turning red in fall
Bloom length:	10 weeks, repeat bloomer
Height:	12 inches **Width/spacing:** 15 inches
Light:	Sun to part shade **Soil:** Average, well-drained
Care:	Deadhead for continued bloom
Uses:	Border, cottage garden, edger, repeat bloom
Propagation:	Division in fall of offshoots
Problems:	Runners—pull back unwanted new plants
Insider's tips:	This is my favorite geranium because the bloom color and plant habit easily combine with all other perennials!
Combines with:	*Phalaris arundinacea, Filipendula ulmaria* 'Aurea', *Campanula carpatica* 'Deep Blue Clips', *Salvia* x *superba* 'Blue Hill', *Helictotrichon sempervirens*

Tiarella 'Iron Butterfly'
IRON BUTTERFLY FOAMFLOWER

Plant type:	Perennial, semi-evergreen **Zone:** 3–8
Flower:	Fragrant white-tinged, pink clusters of tiny star-shaped flowers forming a spike
Foliage:	Light green, very lobed leaves with a distinct dark butterfly in the center
Bloom length:	14-plus weeks, with the possibility of bloom in September and October!
Height:	10–12 inches **Width/spacing:** 12 inches
Light:	Part shade, shade **Soil:** Rich, moist
Care:	Deadhead for neatness and repeat bloom
Uses:	Edger, shade garden, woodland garden, long bloomer, unusual form
Propagation:	Patented plant—do not propagate
Problems:	None
Insider's tips:	I asked breeder Dan Heims of Terra Nova nursery near Portland, Oregon, to recommend his favorite, long-blooming *Tiarella*, and this was it! I can't wait to try it!
Combines with:	*Campanula poscharskyana, Platycodon grandiflorus* 'Sentimental Blue', *Galium odoratum, Brunnera macrophylla, Astilbe japonica* 'Rheinland'

Tradescantia virginiana 'Concord Grape'
CONCORD GRAPE SPIDERWORT

Plant type:	Perennial **Zone:** 4–9
Flower:	Grape-colored, three-petaled, up-facing
Foliage:	Blue-green straps on upright stems
Bloom length:	12-plus weeks
Height:	12–18 inches **Width/spacing:** 18 inches
Light:	Sun to light shade **Soil:** Average, well-drained
Care:	Deadhead for neatness; cut back plant to regenerate fresh foliage
Uses:	Long bloomer, foliage color, cottage garden, mid-border
Propagation:	Division in spring or fall
Problems:	Foliage gets very shabby by August
Insider's tips:	The blue foliage and long bloom are very appealing, but 'Concord Grape' desperately needs cutting back in August and may leave a hole in the fall garden.
Combines with:	*Astilbe japonica* 'Rheinland', *Aquilegia canadensis* 'Corbett', *Campanula carpatica* 'Deep Blue Clips', *Leucanthemum* x *superbum* 'Snowcap', *Coreopsis verticillata* 'Moonbeam'

Adiantum pedatum
MAIDENHAIR FERN

Plant type: Perennial, native, fern   **Zone:** 3–8

Flower: None

Foliage: Bright green fingers along black stems; fronds form an open umbrella

Bloom length: N/A

Height: 12–20 inches   **Width/spacing:** 12 inches

Light: Shade to bright light with no sun

Soil: Rich, moist, slightly acidic

Care: Mulch to retain moisture

Uses: Woodland, naturalizes, unusual foliage effect, water's edge

Propagation: Allow to colonize (does this slowly)

Problems: Take care to not walk on the root zone

Insider's tips: Although ferns do not bloom, they are necessary in the "continuous bloom" shade garden—their lacy texture fills in for bloom.

Combines with: *Hosta* 'Gold Edger', *Astilbe* 'Bridal Veil', *Kirengeshoma palmata*, *Trillium grandiflorum*

Athyrium filix-femina
LADY FERN

Plant type: Perennial, native, fern   **Zone:** 4–9

Flower: None

Foliage: Light green, very lacy

Bloom length: N/A

Height: 30 inches   **Width/spacing:** 24 inches

Light: Part shade to sun   **Soil:** Rich, moist

Care: Mulch to retain soil moisture

Uses: Woodland, structure, wildflower, texture, background, shade garden, water's edge, wet garden

Propagation: Division in spring

Problems: None

Insider's tips: The laciest of the ferns, lady fern is often found next to streams and ponds.

Combines with: *Asarum canadense, Hosta* 'Blue Angel', *Phlox divaricata, Stylophorum diphyllum, Brunnera macrophylla, Arisaema triphyllum*

Athyrium nipponicum 'Pictum'
JAPANESE PAINTED FERN

Plant type:	Perennial, fern **Zone:** 5–8
Flower:	None
Foliage:	Arching fronds, variegated with touches of pink and silver; wine red stems
Bloom length:	N/A
Height:	18 inches **Width/spacing:** 24 inches
Light:	Part shade, shade; prefers morning sun **Soil:** Rich, moist
Care:	Easy
Uses:	Woodland garden, shady garden, bright textural accent
Propagation:	Division in spring
Problems:	None
Insider's tips:	The unusual coloration of this fern makes it very popular for shade gardeners . . . and it's easy, too!
Combines with:	*Astilbe japonica* 'Rhineland', *Galium odoratum, Astilbe simplicifolia* 'Sprite', *Heuchera* 'Plum Pudding', *Hosta* 'Halcyon'

Corydalis lutea
FUMITORY, CORYDALIS, HOLLOWORT

Plant type: Perennial **Zone:** 5–8

Flower: Lemon yellow, pendulous, looks like fringed bleeding heart

Foliage: Light blue-green (glaucous), fernlike

Bloom length: 20-plus weeks

Height: 12 inches **Width/spacing:** 12 inches

Light: Part shade **Soil:** Average, well-drained

Care: You may wish to deadhead periodically for neatness.

Uses: Shade border, rock garden, walls, naturalizes, long bloomer

Propagation: Self-sows; division in spring or fall

Problems: Must have drier, loose soils

Insider's tips: An amazing shade plant that just keeps going and going! The white-flowered sister plant *Corydalis ochroleuca* does the same. (I have not had much luck with the blue-flowered varieties.)

Combines with: *Camassia leichtlinii, Aquilegia canadensis, Hosta ventricosa* 'Aureo-marginata', *Hosta* 'Golden Tiara', *Asarum europaeum*

Dryopteris marginalis
LEATHERWOOD FERN, MARGINAL SHIELD FERN

Plant type: Perennial, native, fern, evergreen **Zone:** 4–8

Flower: None

Foliage: Evergreen, lacy and seemingly delicate wedge-shaped fronds

Bloom length: N/A

Height: 24 inches **Width/spacing:** 36 inches

Light: Shade **Soil:** Rich, moist; tolerates some dryness

Care: Mulch to retain soil moisture

Uses: Woodland, shade garden, wildflower garden

Propagation: Not a spreading fern; best to add to an existing group

Problems: None

Insider's tips: The fronds stay evergreen until June the following year, well after new foliage has filled in. Use leatherwood ferns to replace ostrich ferns, which go dormant in August.

Combines with: *Galium odoratum, Polygonatum commutatum, Stylophorum diphyllum, Brunnera macrophylla*

Nepeta mussinii (N. racemosa) 'Blue Wonder'
CATMINT

Plant type: Perennial, herb **Zone:** 3–7

Flower: Dainty blue flowers that form a frothy spike

Foliage: Gray-green, billowy, mounds, minty fragrance

Bloom length: 6-plus weeks

Height: 12 inches **Width/spacing:** 24 inches, spreading

Light: Full sun **Soil:** Average, well-drained

Care: Cut back hard after bloom for repeat bloom and to diminish self-seeding

Uses: Herb garden, blue garden, edger, cottage garden, rock garden, edge softener

Propagation: Division; cuttings in early summer; self-sows

Problems: Rogue out seedlings

Insider's tips: I often use this catmint in sites where lavender will not grow. The neighbor's cat may take a roll in your catmint but with no ill effect to the plant!

Combines with: *Alchemilla mollis, Geranium sanguineum* var. *striatum, Iris sibirica* 'Caesar's Brother', *Iris pallida* 'Argentea-variegata'

Onoclea sensibilis
SENSITIVE FERN

Plant type:	Perennial, native, fern **Zone:** 3–8
Flower:	None
Foliage:	Light green, rounded leaflets
Bloom length:	N/A
Height:	24–30 inches **Width/spacing:** 30 inches
Light:	Open shade **Soil:** Rich, moist
Care:	Easy
Uses:	Brightens shade, naturalizes, a bolder-textured fern, water's edge
Propagation:	Division in spring
Problems:	None
Insider's tips:	Try using diverse ferns in the shade garden with hostas and woodland natives for textural contrast.
Combines with:	*Actaea rubra, Chelone lyonii, Lobelia cardinalis, Cimicifuga racemosa, Rodgersia aesculifolia, Astilbe chinensis* 'Superba', *Hosta* 'Halcyon'

Osmunda cinnamomea
CINNAMON FERN

Plant type: Perennial, native, fern **Zone:** 3–7

Flower: None

Foliage: Bright green; fertile fronds bearing spore cases appear in the center of plant and are cinnamon-colored.

Bloom length: N/A

Height: 3–6 feet **Width/spacing:** 30 inches

Light: Part shade, shade **Soil:** Rich, moist

Care: Requires more moisture than most ferns

Uses: Woodland, water's edge, bog, wet garden, back of the border

Propagation: Division

Problems: None

Insider's tips: The ultimate height is dependent on proper conditions, particularly the soil moisture. The fertile cinnamon-colored fronds can be left up for winter interest.

Combines with: *Asarum canadense, Hosta* 'Sum and Substance', *Stylophorum diphyllum, Cimicifuga racemosa*

Polystichum acrostichoides
CHRISTMAS FERN

Plant type:	Perennial, native, fern, evergreen **Zone:** 3–9
Flower:	None
Foliage:	Shiny, dark green, evergreen
Bloom length:	N/A
Height:	18–24 inches **Width/spacing:** 24 inches
Light:	Part shade, shade **Soil:** Rich, moist
Care:	Mulch to retain soil moisture
Uses:	Woodland, shade garden, water's edge, Christmas arrangements, winter interest
Propagation:	Slow to colonize
Problems:	Seems slow to increase in cultivated settings
Insider's tips:	Another favorite evergreen fern. It got its name because the fronds can be used in arrangements at Christmastime.
Combines with:	*Epimedium* 'Crimson', *Asarum europaeum*, *Hosta* cultivars, *Polygonatum odoratum* 'Variegatum', *Aruncus aethusifolius*

Polystichum braunii
BRAUN'S HOLLY FERN

Plant type:	Perennial, native, fern **Zone:** 4–8
Flower:	None
Foliage:	More finely divided than most ferns, yet has a bold presence as a plant; semi-evergreen
Bloom length:	N/A
Height:	24–30 inches **Width/spacing:** 30–36 inches
Light:	Part shade, shade **Soil:** Rich, moist
Care:	Easy
Uses:	Naturalizes, woodland, shade garden, wildflower, specimen
Propagation:	Division only from well-established specimens
Problems:	Finding this fern at the nursery
Insider's tips:	The few mail-order catalogues that carry it run out early! Tassel fern (*Polystichum polyblepharum*) looks similar but is harder to establish.
Combines with:	*Hosta* 'Sum and Substance', *Brunnera macrophylla*, *Tricyrtis hirta*, *Cimicifuga simplex*, *Actaea rubra*

Salvia x superba (S. nemerosa) 'May Night'
MEADOW SAGE, PERENNIAL BLUE SALVIA

Plant type:	Perennial, drought-tolerant **Zone:** 5–10
Flower:	Violet-purple, narrow spikes
Foliage:	Compact, aromatic, olive green basal mound
Bloom length:	12 weeks
Height:	15–24 inches **Width/spacing:** 18 inches
Light:	Full sun **Soil:** Average, well-drained
Care:	Easy; deadhead for repeat bloom
Uses:	Long bloomer, herb garden, edger, filler, attracts butterflies
Propagation:	Division in spring or fall
Problems:	Fewer problems with "lodging" (falling away from the center) than other perennial blue salvias
Insider's tips:	'May Night' is the earliest of salvias to bloom. If cut back in June and August after blooms start turning brown, this salvia will flush out a second and third period of bloom.
Combines with:	*Achillea* x 'Anthea', *Geranium sanguineum* var. *striatum*, *Echinacea purpurea* 'Magnus', *Leucanthemum* x *superbum* 'Snowcap'

Aruncus aethusifolius
DWARF GOAT'S BEARD

Plant type:	Perennial **Zone:** 4–8
Flower:	Cream-white tightly clustered on branching stems
Foliage:	Very lacy and delicate mounds of light green, like a fine-textured astilbe
Bloom length:	4–5 weeks
Height:	10 inches **Width/spacing:** 12 inches
Light:	Part shade **Soil:** Rich, moist
Care:	Easy
Uses:	Edger, textural contrast, white garden
Propagation:	Division in the fall after three years
Problems:	None
Insider's tips:	The foliage is almost fernlike. It makes a good contrast with the bold foliage of hostas.
Combines with:	*Hosta* 'Great Expectations', *Polystichum acrostichoides*, *Asarum europaeum*, *Iris cristata* 'Alba', *Lamium maculatum* 'White Nancy'

Aruncus dioicus
GOAT'S BEARD

Plant type:	Perennial, native **Zone:** 3–7
Flower:	Creamy white plumes, showiest on male plant
Foliage:	Stately, divided leaves remind one of a giant astilbe
Bloom length:	4–5 weeks
Height:	3–6 feet **Width/spacing:** 3–4 feet
Light:	Light shade **Soil:** Rich, moist
Care:	Deadhead for neatness and to prevent seeding of female plants
Uses:	Woodland edge, background, wet garden, architectural accent, mixed border, white garden
Propagation:	Not recommended
Problems:	Fewer blooms in shadier sites
Insider's tips:	This is a perennial of shrublike proportions when established, usually at three years. And if it's well grown with consistent soil moisture, the plumes will be spectacular.
Combines with:	*Iris sibirica, Campanula lactiflora, Lilium* cultivars, *Trollius chinensis, Lysimachia punctata, Lobelia siphilitica, Ligularia stenocephala* 'The Rocket'

Astilbe x *arendsii* 'Deutschland'
DEUTSCHLAND ASTILBE, FALSE SPIREA

Plant type:	Perennial **Zone:** 4–9
Flower:	White, tapering plume
Foliage:	Finely cut, glossy, dark green in dense mounds
Bloom length:	2–4 weeks
Height:	24 inches **Width/spacing:** 18 inches
Light:	Part shade; tolerates sun **Soil:** Rich, moist
Care:	Mulch for moisture retention and to increase soil fertility
Uses:	Woodland, water's edge, wet garden, shade garden, cut flower
Propagation:	Division in fall, though I have yet to divide any of my astilbes
Problems:	Dies without proper soil moisture; needs renewed supply of nutrients from extra fertilizer and compost
Insider's tips:	It is worth planning a sequence of bloom of different types of all astilbes—see chart in appendix D. Remember that astilbes are "gross feeders," depleting soils of nutrients.
Combines with:	*Hosta* 'Patriot', *Athyrium nipponicum* 'Pictum', *Heuchera* 'Plum Pudding', *Tiarella* 'Iron Butterfly', shade-tolerant roses like 'Ballerina' or 'Gruss an Auchen'

Astilbe x *arendsii* 'Fanal'
FANAL ASTILBE

Plant type:	Perennial **Zone:** 4–9
Flower:	Dark-red, tight plume with dark stems
Foliage:	Finely cut, glossy green in dense mounds
Bloom length:	2–4 weeks
Height:	18–24 inches **Width/spacing:** 24 inches
Light:	Part shade **Soil:** Rich, moist
Care:	Mulch for moisture retention and to increase soil fertility
Uses:	Woodland, water's edge, wet garden, shade garden, cut flower
Propagation:	Division in fall
Problems:	Can dry out and die
Insider's tips:	Astilbes with ferns are invaluable for deerproofing your shade garden!
Combines with:	*Alchemilla mollis, Amsonia hubrectii, Hosta* 'Gingko Craig', *Onoclea sensibilis*

Astilbe japonica 'Rheinland'
RHEINLAND ASTILBE

Plant type:	Perennial **Zone:** 4–8
Flower:	Light salmon pink upright plumes with blushed red stems
Foliage:	Finely cut, glossy green in dense mounds
Bloom length:	4 weeks
Height:	24 inches **Width/spacing:** 18 inches
Light:	Part shade **Soil:** Rich, moist
Care:	Mulch for moisture retention and to increase soil fertility
Uses:	Woodland, water's edge, wet garden, shade garden, cut flower
Propagation:	Division in spring, but I have yet to divide any of my astilbes
Problems:	Do not allow to dry out
Insider's tips:	Remember, astilbes are "gross feeders," depleting soils of nutrients. Compost and a little extra fertilizer are helpful.
Combines with:	*Alchemilla mollis, Hosta* 'Gold Edger', *Asarum europaeum, Hosta* 'Halcyon', *Athyrium nipponicum* 'Pictum'

Astilbe simplicifolia 'Praecox Alba'
PRAECOX ALBA ASTILBE

Plant type:	Perennial **Zone:** 4–8
Flower:	White, very upright, open plumes
Foliage:	Dark green, glossy, finely cut in loose mounds
Bloom length:	3–5 weeks
Height:	24–30 inches **Width/spacing:** 24 inches
Light:	Part shade **Soil:** Rich, moist
Care:	Mulch for moisture retention and to increase soil fertility
Uses:	Woodland, water's edge, wet garden, shade garden, cut flower
Propagation:	Division in fall
Problems:	If soil is too dry, this astilbe will eventually die.
Insider's tips:	I am not sure that 'Praecox Alba' is a simplicifolia hybrid, as it blooms so early. Simplicifolias usually are late-season bloomers.
Combines with:	*Polystichum braunii, Ligularia stenocephala* 'The Rocket', *Lobelia siphilitica, Myosotis sylvatica*

Campanula lactiflora
MILKY BELLFLOWER

Plant type:	Perennial **Zone:** 4–7
Flower:	Pale lilac-blue, cup-shaped, nodding on slender stems
Foliage:	Bushy
Bloom length:	6–8 weeks
Height:	3–5 feet **Width/spacing:** 3 feet
Light:	Sun to part shade **Soil:** Rich, moist, well-drained
Care:	Cut back stems after bloom to prevent self-sowing and for fall rebloom; stake as necessary
Uses:	Back of border, cottage garden, blue garden
Propagation:	Division after blooming, often self-sows
Problems:	Often needs staking; watch for slugs
Insider's tips:	Other shorter milky bellflowers should be considered as well: 'Pritchard's Variety' and 'Superba'.
Combines with:	*Delphinium* x *elatum, Lilium bulbiferum, Digitalis grandiflora, Phlox maculata* 'Miss Lingard', *Allium aflatunense* 'Purple Sensation', *Hemerocallis* 'Hyperion'

Campanula poscharskyana
SERBIAN BELLFLOWER

Plant type:	Perennial, groundcover, drought-tolerant **Zone:** 3–7
Flower:	Small violet-blue stars on arching or sprawling stems
Foliage:	Creeping, sprawling stems with heart-shaped leaves
Bloom length:	4 weeks, repeats
Height:	6 inches **Width/spacing:** 18 inches
Light:	Sun to part shade **Soil:** Average, well-drained to gritty
Care:	Sheer for repeat bloom
Uses:	Edger, woodland edge, rock garden, cottage garden, window box, groundcover
Propagation:	Division in early spring
Problems:	Gets very lanky in too much shade and eventually dies out
Insider's tips:	A new white-flowered cultivar 'E. H. Frost' is very floriferous and less sprawling than the species.
Combines with:	*Corydalis lutea*, *Digitalis grandiflora*, *Geranium clarkei* 'Kashmir White', *Astilbe simplicifolia* 'Sprite', *Heuchera* 'Plum Pudding'

Crambe cordifolia
SEA KALE, COLEWORT

Plant type:	Perennial **Zone:** 6–9
Flower:	Many branched stems display a cloud of small white flowers, like a giant baby's breath
Foliage:	2-foot-tall mound of lobed and wrinkled leaves
Bloom length:	6 weeks **Height:** 5–7 feet **Width/spacing:** 4 feet
Light:	Sun to light shade
Soil:	Average to rocky, well-drained, somewhat alkaline
Care:	Stake if necessary
Uses:	Architectural accent, background, specimen
Propagation:	Division in spring
Problems:	Marginally hardy in Zone 5—however, I have seen healthy plants in southern Wisconsin; takes up a lot of space
Insider's tips:	Since this plant does not do well in improved garden soils and becomes a huge specimen, it's not found in the average garden.
Combines with:	*Artemisia ludoviciana* 'Valerie Finnis', *Rudbeckia nitida* 'Herbstsonne', *Delphinium* x *elatum*, *Heliopsis helianthoides* 'Summer Sun', *Hemerocallis* 'Tetrina's Daughter'

Digitalis grandiflora (D. ambigua)
YELLOW FOXGLOVE

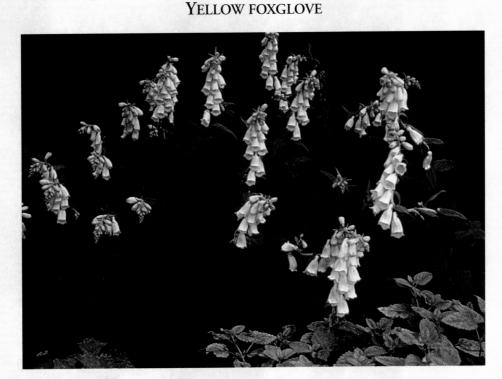

Plant type:	Perennial, herb **Zone:** 3–8
Flower:	Pale yellow, slender, tubular bells in clusters forming a spike
Foliage:	Vertical line (spike) from basal rosette
Bloom length:	6–8 weeks
Height:	24–30 inches **Width/spacing:** 12 inches
Light:	Part shade, part sun **Soil:** Rich, moist, well-drained
Care:	Reblooms with deadheading
Uses:	Cut flower, woodland edge, herb garden, mid-border, architectural accent, cottage garden
Propagation:	Self-sows; transplant seedlings anytime
Problems:	None
Insider's tips:	Although this foxglove only comes in yellow, it is a true perennial that never needs dividing. Bonus seedlings and late season rebloom depend on deadheading practices.
Combines with:	*Lamium maculatum* 'Beedham's White', *Campanula glomerata* 'Superba', *Dicentra spectabilis, Aconitum* x *cammarum* 'Newry Blue', *Iris sibirica* 'Caesar's Brother', *Iris tectorum*

Helictotrichon sempervirens
BLUE OAT GRASS

Plant type:	Ornamental grass, evergreen **Zone:** 4–8
Flower:	Airy, wheatlike
Foliage:	Striking blue leaves arching to form mounds
Bloom length:	4-plus weeks
Height:	24 inches **Width/spacing:** 24 inches
Light:	Full sun **Soil:** Average, well-drained
Care:	Trim out inflorescence to retain good blue effect; cut back in late winter
Uses:	Mixed border, cottage garden, winter interest, soft texture, foliage color, accent
Propagation:	Division in early spring
Problems:	None
Insider's tips:	This is my favorite ornamental grass for the blue foliage color and the length of time that color is retained in the garden—until March of the following year in the Midwest!
Combines with:	*Sedum* x 'Autumn Joy', *Heuchera* 'Plum Pudding', *Rosa* 'Carefree Wonder', *Rosa* 'Flower Carpet', *Phlox paniculata* 'Bright Eyes', *Callirhoe involucrata*, *Geranium sanguineum* var. *striatum*

Hemerocallis 'Pink Lavender Appeal'
PINK LAVENDER APPEAL DAYLILY

Plant type: Perennial   **Zone:** 3–8

Flower: Pale lavender-pink, six-petaled lily with a greenish yellow throat

Foliage: Straplike leaves forming a neat fountainlike mound

Bloom length: 6 weeks

Height: 26–30 inches   **Width/spacing:** 30 inches

Light: Sun to light shade   **Soil:** Average, well-drained

Care: Deadhead for neatness

Uses: Cottage garden, mixed border, cut flower

Propagation: Division every three years in spring or fall

Problems: Earwigs

Insider's tips: Pink and white daylilies have become very popular, adding a broader dimension to a genus we usually think of as yellow and orange.

Combines with: *Veronica spicata* 'Blue Charm', *Lamium maculatum* 'Pink Pewter', *Phlox paniculata* 'David', *Rosa* 'Betty Prior', *Platycodon grandiflorus* 'Mariesii'

Hosta sieboldiana 'Frances Williams'
FRANCES WILLIAMS HOSTA

Plant type:	Perennial **Zone:** 3–9
Flower:	White-tinged lavender drooping lilies
Foliage:	Bold, circular, blue-green leaves with lime green edges
Bloom length:	4 weeks
Height:	24 inches **Width/spacing:** 36–40 inches
Light:	Part shade, shade **Soil:** Rich, moist, well-drained
Care:	Easy
Uses:	Massed, mixed hosta border, edger, shade garden, cut flower
Propagation:	Division in spring
Problems:	Sometimes slugs, deer-browse
Insider's tips:	This hosta was one of the first variegated selections and remains a favorite with new gardeners.
Combines with:	*Epimedium* x *versicolor* 'Sulphureum', *Cimicifuga racemosa, Onoclea sensibilis, Lamium maculatum* 'Beedham's White'

Lavandula angustifolia 'Hidcote'
HIDCOTE ENGLISH LAVENDER

Plant type:	Perennial, herb **Zone:** 5–9
Flower:	Small, blue-purple clusters forming a tight spike
Foliage:	Gray-green, aromatic, fine, needlelike
Bloom length:	4–6 weeks
Height:	18 inches **Width/spacing:** 18 inches
Light:	Full sun **Soil:** Average to poor, sandy, well-drained
Care:	Cut back to 6 inches in spring
Uses:	Herb garden, edger, cottage garden, formal edger, fragrance, blue garden, gray contrast
Propagation:	Division spring or fall
Problems:	Rots out with too much rain and humidity; not tolerant of clay soils
Insider's tips:	Planting along stone or brick paths laid in sand is an ideal place for lavender!
Combines with:	Roses, *Geranium endressii* 'Wargrave Pink', *Coreopsis grandiflora* 'Sunray', *Hemerocallis* 'Happy Returns', *Dianthus* x *allwoodii* 'Doris'

Lilium cultivars (Asiatic hybrids)
ASIATIC LILY

Plant type:	Bulb **Zone:** 4–8
Flower:	Clusters of buds open to upward or out-facing flowers, petals often spotted
Foliage:	Upright stems with whorled glossy lance-shaped leaves
Bloom length:	4–6 weeks (dependent on the number of buds; mature plants have most buds)
Height:	30 inches **Width/spacing:** 18 inches
Light:	Sun to light shade **Soil:** Average, well-drained
Care:	Well-drained soil is a must!
Uses:	Interplant in border, architectural accent, showy, cottage garden
Propagation:	Division after foliage has "ripened"
Problems:	Rabbit-browse; rots in overly wet soil
Insider's tips:	I love using lilies as exclamation marks throughout the garden.
Combines with:	*Leucanthemum* x *superbum* 'Ryan's White', *Salvia* x *superba* 'May Night', *Veronica* 'Sunny Border Blue', *Malva alcea*, *Phlox maculata* 'Miss Lingard'

Lilium regale 'Album'
REGAL LILY

Plant type:	Bulb **Zone:** 5–8
Flower:	White with yellow throat, funnel-shaped, fragrant
Foliage:	Upright stems with lance-shaped leaves
Bloom length:	3 week
Height:	3–4 feet **Width/spacing:** 12 inches
Light:	Sun to light shade
Soil:	Average, well-drained; drainage is crucial
Care:	Fertilize before and after bloom; deadhead for neatness
Uses:	Border, cottage garden, evening (moonlight) garden, structural, fragrance, cut flower
Propagation:	Allow to colonize
Problems:	Rabbits love it
Insider's tips:	Deadhead for neatness, but leave at least two-thirds of the stem with leaves to nourish bulbs for next year's bloom!
Combines with:	*Tanacetum parthenium* 'Aureum', *Heliopsis helianthoides* 'Summer Sun', *Geranium* x *magnificum*, *Hemerocallis*, *Coreopsis grandiflora* 'Sunray', *Campanula lactiflora*

Oenothera fruticosa ssp. *glauca (O. tetragona)*
SUNDROPS

Plant type:	Perennial, native **Zone:** 4–8
Flower:	Bright yellow poppy shape from red bud
Foliage:	Dark green, spreading basal rosette to upright stems; red fall color
Bloom length:	4 weeks
Height:	18–20 inches **Width/spacing:** 18 inches
Light:	Sun to part shade **Soil:** Average, well-drained
Care:	Be prepared to control spreading, although basal rosettes are easily pulled out
Uses:	Meadow, cottage garden, yellow that brightens a garden, mid-border
Propagation:	Division after blooming
Problems:	None
Insider's tips:	Those spreading rosettes make for good "pass along" plants to friends and neighbors. I have pushed the light tolerance by successfully growing sundrops in part shade.
Combines with:	*Alchemilla mollis, Salvia* x *superba* 'May Night', *Artemisia ludoviciana* 'Valerie Finnis', *Centaurea montana, Campanula glomerata* 'Superba'

Penstemon digitalis 'Husker's Red'
BEARD TONGUE

Plant type:	Perennial **Zone:** 4–8
Flower:	White with pink-tinged bells forming a spike
Foliage:	Bronzed green to burgundy; upright
Bloom length:	5 weeks
Height:	30–36 inches **Width/spacing:** 30 inches
Light:	Full sun **Soil:** Average, well-drained
Care:	If plant declines after blooming, cut back to basal rosette
Uses:	Border, foliage color, rock garden, cut flower, attracts butterflies
Propagation:	Division in fall
Problems:	Seedlings may revert to species and lose burgundy color in the foliage
Insider's tips:	Seed heads provide good late season burgundy color. A University of Nebraska selection, this is the best for the moisture-retentive soils of the Midwest.
Combines with:	*Campanula carpatica* 'Deep Blue Clips', *Veronica spicata* 'Blue Charm', *Geranium* x *magnificum*, *Geranium* x *cantabrigiense* 'Biokovo'

Phlomis fruticosa
JERUSALEM SAGE

Plant type: Perennial, herb, drought-tolerant   **Zone:** 4–8

Flower: Layered whorls of yellow flowers on woody stems

Foliage: Gray-green, heart-shaped leaves from tall, felted mounds

Bloom length: 4–6 weeks

Height: 30–36 inches   **Width/spacing:** 18 inches

Light: Full sun, afternoon shade in the South

Soil: Average to poor, well-drained

Care: Treat as a Mediterranean plant

Uses: Herb garden, cottage garden, mid-border, architectural accent

Propagation: Division in spring or fall

Problems: Rots with too much moisture

Insider's tips: This is a highly favored plant in England—less so in the United States, perhaps due to difficulties in meeting the plants' soil requirements.

Combines with: *Heliopsis helianthoides* 'Summer Sun', *Campanula lactiflora*, *Iris sibirica* 'Caesar's Brother', *Malva moschata* 'Alba', *Hemerocallis* 'Ice Carnival', *Geranium* x *magnificum*

Phlox maculata (carolina) 'Miss Lingard'

WEDDING PHLOX, SPOTTED PHLOX

Plant type: Perennial   **Zone:** 3–9

Flower: White with yellow eye, clustered and more columnar than other border phlox

Foliage: Shiny, lance-shaped leaves on upright stems

Bloom length: 5–6 weeks

Height: 24–30 inches   **Width/spacing:** 18 inches

Light: Full sun   **Soil:** Rich, moist, well-drained

Care: Easy, does not need staking, deadhead for neatness

Uses: Mid-border, fragrance, cottage garden, early border phlox

Propagation: Division of offshoots in spring

Problems: None

Insider's tips: 'Miss Lingard' starts the season for border phlox and works well to offset other bright flower colors.

Combines with: *Monarda didyma* 'Gardenview Scarlet', *Salvia verticillata* 'Purple Rain', *Hemerocallis* 'Happy Returns', *Geranium* x *magnificum*, *Oenothera fruticosa* ssp. *glauca*

Rodgersia aesculifolia
RODGER'S FLOWER, FINGERLEAF RODGERSIA

Plant type:	Perennial **Zone:** 5–8
Flower:	Fragrant, tiny, cream to creamy pink, branching into flat-topped clusters
Foliage:	Green—sometimes bronzed—leaves resembling a horse-chestnut tree
Bloom length:	6–7 weeks
Height:	3–4 feet **Width/spacing:** 24–30 inches
Light:	Sun to part shade **Soil:** Rich, moist
Care:	Maintain moisture in soil
Uses:	Specimen, water's edge, wet garden, woodland edge, architectural accent, bold foliage
Propagation:	Division in spring
Problems:	Looks terrible without consistent moisture
Insider's tips:	Many gardeners think they have "wet" gardens in the spring, but these sites usually dry out by summer and do not provide the consistent soil moisture required.
Combines with:	*Lysimachia punctata, Hosta* 'Sum and Substance', *Iris pseudacorus, Astilbe* x *arendsii* 'Fanal', *Onoclea sensibilis*

Stachys byzantina 'Helene von Stein'
LAMB'S EARS

Plant type:	Perennial, groundcover **Zone:** 4–8
Flower:	An occasional pink, furry spike
Foliage:	Large gray-green and felted leaves in mounds; evergreen in milder climates
Bloom length:	Sporadic
Height:	8 inches **Width/spacing:** 12 inches, spreading
Light:	Full sun **Soil:** Average to poor, well-drained
Care:	Deadhead to keep neat
Uses:	Groundcover, front of border, foliage color, easy care, edging
Propagation:	Division in spring
Problems:	May "melt out" in humid, wet summers
Insider's tips:	'Helene von Stein'—sometimes called 'Big Ears'—has larger leaves than the species with little bloom. It is primarily grown for its foliage color. Another nonflowering choice might be *Stachys byzantina* 'Silver Carpet'.
Combines with:	*Hemerocallis* 'Rocket City', *Iris tectorum, Rosa* 'Carefree Wonder', *Salvia* x *superba* 'May Night', *Campanula glomerata, Coreopsis grandiflora* 'Sunray'

Stachys macrantha 'Superba'

BIG BETONY

Plant type:	Perennial **Zone:** 2–8
Flower:	Whorls of violet-rose along a spiky stem
Foliage:	Dark green clumps of scalloped ovals
Bloom length:	6 weeks, some repeat in fall
Height:	24 inches **Width/spacing:** 24 inches
Light:	Sun to part shade; some shade needed in the South
Soil:	Average, well-drained
Care:	Easy; deadhead for neatness
Uses:	Edger, mid-border, spiky contrast, cottage garden
Propagation:	Division in fall
Problems:	Flowers best in cooler regions
Insider's tips:	The flower color needs companions that blend it in. But it is easy to care for and reliable in well-drained soils.
Combines with:	*Alchemilla mollis, Campanula lactiflora, Tanacetum parthenium* 'Aureum', *Phlox maculata* 'Miss Lingard'

Thalictrum flavum 'Glaucum' (*T. speciosissimum*)
DUSTY MEADOWRUE

Plant type: Perennial   **Zone:** 5–8

Flower: Fuzzy, yellow panicle on top of tall stems

Foliage: Many small, scalloped, blue-green leaves on upright plant

Bloom length: 4 weeks

Height: 5 feet   **Width/spacing:** 24 inches

Light: Sun to light shade   **Soil:** Rich, moist

Care: Deadhead for neatness

Uses: Architectural accent, background, foliage color, cottage garden, cut flower

Propagation: Division in fall

Problems: May need staking

Insider's tips: I would love this plant even if it didn't bloom! The foliage is also used for flower arrangements.

Combines with: *Clematis* 'Jackmani', *Iris sibirica* 'Caesar's Brother', *Alchemilla mollis*, *Hemerocallis* 'Tetrina's Daughter'

Veronica 'Minuet'
MINUET WOOLLY SPEEDWELL

Plant type: Perennial **Zone:** 3–8

Flower: Pink spike

Foliage: Silver, hairy, oblong leaves forming creeping mat

Bloom length: 4–6 weeks

Height: 12–15 inches **Width/spacing:** 12 inches

Light: Full sun **Soil:** Average to poor, well-drained

Care: Cut off flower stems that flop; maintain good drainage

Uses: Foliage color, edger, cottage garden, rock garden, attracts butterflies

Propagation: Stem cuttings

Problems: None

Insider's tips: The flower spikes are more upright and less susceptible to rot than *Veronica incana*, which has blue flowers.

Combines with: *Campanula carpatica* 'Deep Blue Clips' or 'White Clips', *Hemerocallis* 'Ice Carnival', *Leucanthemum* x *superbum* 'Snowcap'

Achillea sibirica var. *kamtschatica*
SIBERIAN YARROW

Plant type:	Perennial **Zone:** 4–8
Flower:	Lilac-pink clusters forming a flat platelike head 4 inches in diameter
Foliage:	Glossy, dark green, needlelike on upright stems
Bloom length:	10 weeks
Height:	30 inches **Width/spacing:** 18 inches
Light:	Sun to light shade **Soil:** Average, well-drained
Care:	Deadhead for aesthetics and some repeat bloom
Uses:	Cottage garden, herb garden, mid-border, long bloomer
Propagation:	Division in spring or fall
Problems:	Difficult to find
Insider's tips:	I prefer the habit of this plant to *Achillea millefolium* types, which are floppy and can be invasive.
Combines with:	*Allium senescens* var. *glaucum*, *Thymus* x *citriodorus* 'Aureus', *Phlox paniculata* 'Fairest One', *Salvia* x *superba* 'May Night', *Euphorbia myrsinites*, *Artemisia ludoviciana* 'Valerie Finnis'

Asclepias tuberosa
BUTTERFLY WEED

Plant type:	Perennial, native, herb **Zone:** 3–9
Flower:	Fragrant, bright orange flowers that cluster into a rounded shape; ornamental seedpods
Foliage:	Clump-forming, rough leaves
Bloom length:	8–10 weeks
Height:	18–30 inches **Width/spacing:** 15 inches
Light:	Full sun **Soil:** Average, well-drained, sandy
Care:	Thrives on neglect
Uses:	Prairie/meadow, wildflower, attracts butterflies and hummingbirds, bright color accent
Propagation:	Difficult to transplant; slow from seed
Problems:	Late to break dormancy in spring
Insider's tips:	I like to bring this native prairie plant into the garden as a bright color accent. The new cultivar 'Gay Butterflies' is worth trying for its range of colors: yellow, orange, and red.
Combines with:	*Salvia verticillata* 'Purple Rain', *Artemisia ludoviciana* 'Valerie Finnis', *Delphinium grandiflorum* 'Blue Butterfly', *Gaillardia* x *grandiflora* 'Goblin', *Campanula carpatica* 'Deep Blue Clips', *Echinacea purpurea* 'White Swan', *Buddleia davidii* 'Royal Red'

Astrantia major
MASTERWORT

Plant type:	Perennial **Zone:** 4–7
Flower:	1-inch dome, tinged pink with starlike collar or bract
Foliage:	Mid-green, mounded, maplelike leaves
Bloom length:	6 weeks, off and on **Height:** 30 inches
Width/spacing:	18–20 inches
Light:	Part shade to sun **Soil:** Average to rich, evenly moist
Care:	Deadhead as necessary
Uses:	Cottage garden, dried flower, mid-border, cut flower
Propagation:	Division in spring; self-sows
Problems:	Takes a while to get established; does not tolerate dryness or too much shade
Insider's tips:	*Astrantia major* 'Lars' and 'Hadspen Blood' are cultivars with profuse, dark red blooms.
Combines with:	*Stachys byzantina, Lobelia siphilitica, Lamium maculatum* 'Beedham's White', *Geranium* x *magnificum, Alchemilla mollis*

Callirhoe involucrata
LITTLE WINE CUPS, PURPLE POPPY MALLOW

Plant type:	Perennial **Zone:** 4–7
Flower:	Wine-red poppy
Foliage:	Hardy geranium-like leaves on trailing stems
Bloom length:	12-plus weeks
Height:	6–12 inches **Width/spacing:** 2-plus feet (trailing)
Light:	Full sun **Soil:** Average, well-drained to sandy
Care:	Cut back hard if it's too aggressive a trailer
Uses:	Long bloomer, rock garden, edger, cottage garden
Propagation:	Easy from seed
Problems:	Will not tolerate wet conditions; clambers over surrounding plants
Insider's tips:	If you like plants to be neat and tidy, wine cups is not the plant for you! It clambers over everything in its path, and cutting it back slows up the profuse bloom.
Combines with:	*Leucanthemum* x *superbum* 'Snowcap', *Helictotrichon sempervirens*, *Salvia* x *superba* 'May Night', *Hemerocallis* 'Happy Returns'

Cephalaria gigantea
GIANT SCABIOUS

Plant type:	Perennial **Zone:** 3–8
Flower:	Light yellow; scabiosa-like
Foliage:	Clumps of dark green, coarsely divided foliage with widely branching tall stems; somewhat vase shaped
Bloom length:	6 weeks
Height:	5–6 feet **Width/spacing:** 2–3 feet
Light:	Sun to light shade **Soil:** Average, well-drained
Care:	Generally does not need staking
Uses:	Architectural accent, back of the border, mixed border, cottage garden
Propagation:	Self-sows
Problems:	Overabundant self-sowing; deadhead to prevent "seeding about"
Insider's tips:	A nice "see through" plant to be used as an exclamation mark! It's best seen with a dark green background.
Combines with:	*Achillea* 'Moonshine' *Campanula lactiflora, Alcea rosea, Lilium* x 'Casablanca', *Miscanthus sinensis* 'Strictus'

Heuchera 'Plum Pudding'
PLUM PUDDING CORAL BELLS

Plant type:	Perennial, evergreen **Zone:** 3–9
Flower:	White, open, airy clusters of very tiny bells on long purple stems
Foliage:	Burgundy, mounded, lobed, maplelike leaves; often ever-burgundy
Bloom length:	8–12 weeks
Height:	18 inches **Width/spacing:** 18 inches
Light:	Part shade **Soil:** Rich, moist, well-drained
Care:	Remove previous year's dried leaves and any woody growth as new foliage opens
Uses:	Foliage color, rock garden, edger, winter interest, border blender, cut flower
Propagation:	Division in spring or fall
Problems:	May heave in the winter; if grown with too much afternoon sun, scorching is a problem.
Insider's tips:	I love all the burgundy and purple-leafed hybrids, as they add color to the winter landscape. Don't overlook the blooms, as they work like baby's breath in flower arrangements.
Combines with:	*Astilbe japonica* 'Rheinland', *Astilbe simplicifolia* 'Sprite', *Hemerocallis* 'Raspberry Wine', *Pennisetum alopecuroides*, *Campanula poscharskyana*, *Athyrium nipponicum* 'Pictum'

Heuchera 'Smokey Rose'
SMOKEY ROSE CORAL BELLS

Plant type:	Perennial, evergreen **Zone:** 4–9
Flower:	Rosy pink, airy clusters of bells on long arching dark stems
Foliage:	Smokey-green, scalloped, heart-shaped leaves mounded from basal crown
Bloom length:	9–10 weeks
Height:	12–18 inches **Width/spacing:** 15 inches
Light:	Part shade **Soil:** Rich, moist, well-drained
Care:	Deadhead for repeat bloom
Uses:	Rock garden, edger, cut flower, cottage garden, prolific blooms
Propagation:	Division in spring or fall
Problems:	May heave in the winter—mound soil around roots if this happens.
Insider's tips:	'Smokey Rose' is like a never-ending bouquet in the garden—the more you cut, the more it blooms. Friend Barbara Miller highlights this coral bells with yellow flowers and chartreuse foliage.
Combines with:	*Rosa* 'Flower Carpet', *Iris tectorum, Digitalis grandiflora, Hosta* 'Piedmont Gold', *Hemerocallis* 'Summer Wine'

Leucanthemum (*Chrysanthemum*) x *superbum* 'Snowcap'
SNOWCAP SHASTA DAISY

Plant type:	Perennial **Zone:** 4–9
Flower:	Prolific white daisy with a yellow center
Foliage:	Dwarf Shasta foliage with glossy, dark green basal rosette
Bloom length:	8–10 weeks
Height:	15 inches **Width/spacing:** 18 inches
Light:	Full sun **Soil:** Average, well-drained
Care:	Deadhead for repeat bloom and neatness
Uses:	Edger, front of the border, cottage garden, formal garden, long bloomer
Propagation:	Division in spring every other year to remove woody centers
Problems:	Sometimes prone to slugs when not fully established; may heave in winter
Insider's tips:	The dwarf forms of Shasta daisy do not flop all over their neighboring plants.
Combines with:	*Hemerocallis* 'Happy Returns', *Delphinium grandiflorum* 'Blue Butterfly', *Callirhoe involucrata*, *Geranium sanguineum* var. *striatum*, *Platycodon grandiflorus* 'Sentimental Blue', *Veronica alpina* 'Goodness Grows'

Lychnis chalcedonica
MALTESE CROSS

Plant type:	Perennial **Zone:** 3–7
Flower:	Small, scarlet red, cross-shaped individual flowers clustered to form dense rounded heads
Foliage:	Dark green, lancelike leaves on upright stems
Bloom length:	8-plus weeks, occasional repeat into fall
Height:	30–36 inches **Width/spacing:** 18–24 inches
Light:	Sun to light shade **Soil:** Average, moist, well-drained
Care:	Sometimes needs staking
Uses:	Bold color accent, cottage garden, mid-border
Propagation:	Division in spring
Problems:	When excessively dry, leaves become brown and unsightly; cut back to regenerate new growth.
Insider's tips:	The scarlet red flower color causes many gardeners to overlook this plant, but with a little creativity in combining, it can become a wonderfully bright accent.
Combines with:	*Alchemilla mollis, Helictotrichon sempervirens, Campanula glomerata* 'Superba', *Tradescantia* x *andersoniana* 'Zwanenburg Blue', *Gaillardia* x *grandiflora* 'Goblin'

Lychnis coronaria
ROSE CAMPION

Plant type:	Perennial **Zone:** 4–7
Flower:	Very hot pink to fuchsia, 1-inch bloom, on the ends of many-branched stems
Foliage:	Silvery-gray felted, basal crown, branched silvery stems are candelabra-like
Bloom length:	6 weeks
Height:	24–30 inches **Width/spacing:** 18 inches
Light:	Full sun **Soil:** Average to poor, well-drained
Care:	Deadheading prolongs bloom, allow some seeding to renew planting
Uses:	Foliage color, striking color combination, mid-border, cottage garden
Propagation:	Self-sows in light soils
Problems:	Rots in wet soils; not long-lived; doesn't always come up where expected
Insider's tips:	This old-fashioned plant is not often used. It seeds itself into the garden site where it is happiest.
Combines with:	*Phlox paniculata* 'Spring Pearl Series', *Monarda didyma* 'Marshall's Delight', *Salvia* x *superba* 'May Night', *Hemerocallis* 'Raspberry Wine', *Playtcodon grandiflorus* 'Mariesii'

Monarda didyma 'Gardenview Scarlet'
GARDENVIEW SCARLET BEE BALM

Plant type: Perennial   **Zone:** 3–9

Flower: Richer red and larger than cultivar 'Cambridge Scarlet'

Foliage: Mildew-resistant, mintlike fragrance

Bloom length: 6 weeks

Height: 36 inches   **Width/spacing:** 24 inches

Light: Sun to part shade   **Soil:** Average to poor, well-drained

Care: Contain or pull out unwanted shoots

Uses: Mid-border, prairie/meadow, attracts butterflies and humming-birds, cottage garden, herb garden

Propagation: Division in spring every three years to regenerate

Problems: Aggressive spreader

Insider's tips: Another new red bee balm, 'Jacob Cline', is touted as having even larger blooms plus mildew resistance.

Combines with: *Helictotrichon sempervirens, Leucanthemum* x *superbum* 'Ryan's White', *Veronica spicata* 'Blue Charm'

Monarda didyma 'Marshall's Delight'

MARSHALL'S DELIGHT BEE BALM

Plant type:	Perennial **Zone:** 3–9
Flower:	Showy, bright pink, spidery bracts; very free flowering
Foliage:	Mildew-resistant, mint fragrance
Bloom length:	6–8 weeks
Height:	36–40 inches **Width/spacing:** 24 inches
Light:	Sun to part shade **Soil:** Rich, moist
Care:	To contain, pull back spreading stolons; deadhead to lengthen bloom time
Uses:	Mid-border, prairie/meadow, attracts butterflies and humming-birds, cottage garden, herb garden
Propagation:	Divide every three years to regenerate; division any time; cuttings in spring root readily
Problems:	Spreads aggressively by stoloniferous runners
Insider's tips:	The bright array of *Monarda* colors are hard to resist and should be tempered by the amount of work needed to keep this spreader under control. Always choose mildew-resistant varieties!
Combines with:	*Salvia* x *superba* 'May Night', *Echinacea purpurea* 'White Swan', *Kalimeris pinnatifida*, *Hemerocallis* 'Ice Carnival'

Monarda didyma 'Raspberry Wine'
RASPBERRY WINE BEE BALM

Plant type:	Perennial **Zone:** 3–9
Flower:	Wine red, spidery bracts
Foliage:	Dark green, upright habit; fragrant
Bloom length:	6–8 weeks
Height:	36–40 inches **Width/spacing:** 24 inches, spreading
Light:	Sun to light shade **Soil:** Average, well-drained
Care:	Deadheading does not result in much rebloom
Uses:	Mid-border, prairie/meadow, attracts butterflies and humming-birds, cottage garden, herb garden
Propagation:	Division in spring every three years to remove dead centers
Problems:	May need staking; invasive
Insider's tips:	While this plant is mildew resistant, remember that mildew resistance is a relative term—what is resistant in one garden may not be in another!
Combines with:	*Nepeta sibirica, Phlox paniculata* 'David', *Phlox paniculata* 'Eva Cullum', *Lilium* x 'Casablanca'

Nepeta sibirica
SIBERIAN CATMINT

Plant type:	Perennial **Zone:** 4–8
Flower:	Many blue, tubular trumpets forming a spike
Foliage:	Lightly gray-green, sprawling stems are taller and less fragrant than other catmints
Bloom length:	6–10 weeks
Height:	2 feet **Width/spacing:** 24–30 inches
Light:	Sun to light shade **Soil:** Average, well-drained
Care:	Deadhead for repeat bloom
Uses:	Spiky contrast, long bloomer, blue garden, cottage garden
Propagation:	Division; cuttings in early summer
Problems:	Allow space to recline; invasive in rich soils
Insider's tips:	Gardeners who understand the more-sprawling habit can plan ahead as to how and when to incorporate this catmint in the garden.
Combines with:	*Monarda didyma* 'Gardenview Scarlet', *Leucanthemum vulgare*, *Lychnis chalcedonica, Lychnis coronaria*

Tanacetum (Chrysanthemum) parthenium 'Aureum'
GOLDEN FEVERFEW

Plant type:	Perennial, herb **Zone:** 4–9
Flower:	Creamy white, buttonlike tiny mum
Foliage:	Chartreuse-yellow, ferny, mounded with a pungent odor
Bloom length:	6 weeks
Height:	12 inches **Width/spacing:** 15 inches
Light:	Sun to part shade **Soil:** Average, well-drained
Care:	Deadhead for repeat bloom
Uses:	Foliage color, cottage garden, herb garden, cut flower, filler plant
Propagation:	Self-sows; division in spring or fall
Problems:	Deadheading prevents excessive "seeding about"
Insider's tips:	My plants came from seeds given to me in the Cotswold region of England ten years ago. And every year I pass along my seeds to someone else. The foliage is always a standout in the garden.
Combines with:	*Sedum alboroseum* 'Medio-variegatum', *Salvia* x *superba* 'May Night', *Asclepias tuberosa, Aster novae-angliae* 'Purple Dome', *Campanula carpatica* 'Deep Blue Clips', *Campanula glomerata* 'Superba'

Tradescantia x *andersoniana* 'Zwanenberg Blue'
ZWANENBERG BLUE SPIDERWORT

Plant type: Perennial **Zone:** 5–9

Flower: Clear blue, large, three-petaled, closes in heat; flowers close by late afternoon

Foliage: Long, narrow straplike leaves

Bloom length: 6 weeks

Height: 24–30 inches **Width/spacing:** 30 inches, spreading

Light: Sun to part shade

Soil: Rich, moist, well-drained; tolerates other conditions

Care: When foliage turns brown after first bloom, cut back to ground.

Uses: Woodland edge, water's edge, wet garden, attracts butterflies

Propagation: Division in spring or fall

Problems: May be invasive; usually needs renovation cutback

Insider's tips: After renovation cutback, new foliage will be shorter and you can expect a fall rebloom. Site your spiderworts where the empty space left from renovation does not show.

Combines with: *Campanula lactiflora* 'Alba', *Lychnis chalcedonica, Asclepias tuberosa, Leucanthemum* x *superbum* 'Aglaia', *Coreopsis grandiflora* 'Sunray'

Verbena canadensis 'Homestead Purple'

CREEPING VERVAIN, ROSE VERBENA

Plant type:	Perennial, herb **Zone:** 6–9
Flower:	Rosy-purple, pompom-like clusters
Foliage:	Trailing stems with finely cut leaves
Bloom length:	8–10 weeks, repeating
Height:	8 inches **Width/spacing:** 24 inches
Light:	Full sun **Soil:** Average to poor, well-drained
Care:	Deadhead for neatness
Uses:	Edger, weaver, long bloomer, herb garden, cottage garden, attracts butterflies
Propagation:	Division in spring; may reseed
Problems:	Sometimes dies out
Insider's tips:	There have been years when this verbena has wintered over in my Zone 5 garden, but most years I just replace it. Perhaps I should try overwintering it in pots brought into my garage?
Combines with:	*Heuchera* 'Plum Pudding', *Iris pallida* 'Argentea-variegata', *Artemisia stelleriana* 'Silver Brocade', *Geranium sanguineum* var. *striatum*, *Origanum vulgare* 'Aureum'

Veronica 'Sunny Border Blue'
SUNNY BORDER BLUE VERONICA, SPEEDWELL

Plant type: Perennial   **Zone:** 5–8

Flower: Violet-blue spike

Foliage: Shiny ovals on upright stems

Bloom length: 14 weeks

Height: 24 inches   **Width/spacing:** 20 inches

Light: Full sun, tolerates a little shade   **Soil:** Rich, moist, well-drained

Care: Deadhead for reblooming

Uses: Mid-border, blue garden, meadow, long bloomer, attracts butterflies

Propagation: Division spring or fall

Problems: With cool/wet conditions may need to use a fungicidal soap

Insider's tips: I am still looking for the "perfect" veronica that is disease resistant and doesn't flop. 'Sunny Border Blue' comes pretty close, as it's normally mildew and black spot resistant.

Combines with: *Achillea ptarmica, Geranium sanguineum* var. *striatum, Rudbeckia fulgida* var. *sullivantii* 'Goldsturm', *Pennisetum alopecuroides, Phlox paniculata* 'Bright Eyes', *Phlox maculata* 'Miss Lingard', *Echinacea purpurea* 'Magnus'

Achillea x 'Anthea'
ANTHEA YARROW

Plant type:	Perennial **Zone:** 4–8
Flower:	Flat, platelike clusters of pale yellow flowers
Foliage:	Lacy silver mounds
Bloom length:	8–10 weeks
Height:	24–30 inches **Width/spacing:** 24 inches
Light:	Full sun **Soil:** Average to poor, well-drained
Care:	Deadhead into basal mound for neatness and repeat bloom
Uses:	Rock garden, cottage garden, herb garden, mid-border, foliage color, dried flower
Propagation:	Division in spring every two years; discard center
Problems:	Rots with too much water
Insider's tips:	With delayed cold, 'Anthea' may bloom well into October!
Combines with:	*Leucanthemum* x *superbum* 'Snowcap', *Heuchera* 'Plum Pudding', *Salvia* x *superba* 'May Night', *Callirhoe involucrata*, *Campanula glomerata* 'Superba'

Achillea 'Moonshine'
MOONSHINE YARROW

Plant type:	Perennial **Zone:** 3–9
Flower:	Flat, platelike clusters of yellow flowers
Foliage:	Lacy, silver mounds
Bloom length:	6–8 weeks with rebloom if deadheaded
Height:	24 inches **Width/spacing:** 18–24 inches
Light:	Full sun **Soil:** Average to poor, well-drained
Care:	Deadhead for repeat bloom; do not excessively water
Uses:	Rock garden, herb garden, mid-border, foliage color, dried flower
Propagation:	Division in spring every two years; discard center
Problems:	Rots in wet clay soils
Insider's tips:	I prefer the silvery mound-formers in the *Achillea* genus because they are not disease-prone, do not flop, and are not aggressive spreaders.
Combines with:	*Tanacetum parthenium* 'Aureum', *Echinacea purpurea* 'White Swan', *Veronica* 'Sunny Border Blue', *Salvia* x *superba* 'May Night'

Coreopsis grandiflora 'Sunray'
COREOPSIS, TICKSEED

Plant type:	Perennial, drought-tolerant **Zone:** 4–10
Flower:	2-inch semi-double, golden daisy
Foliage:	Compact, mounded form of a popular old-fashioned coreopsis
Bloom length:	12 weeks
Height:	18–20 inches **Width/spacing:** 18 inches
Light:	Sun to light shade **Soil:** Average, well-drained
Care:	Needs frequent deadheading
Uses:	Edger, rock garden, cottage garden, border
Propagation:	Buy new plants
Problems:	Not long-lived
Insider's tips:	Compact forms of coreopsis are much sought after in today's gardens. This one is short-lived, perhaps blooming itself to death. It's well worth replacing!
Combines with:	*Liatris spicata* 'Kobold', *Salvia* x *superba* 'Blue Hill', *Lavandula angustifolia* 'Hidcote', *Echinacea purpurea* 'White Swan', *Delphinium grandiflorum* 'Blue Butterfly'

Delphinium x *elatum*
DELPHINIUM

Plant type:	Perennial **Zone:** 3–7
Flower:	Looks like outfacing blue roses tightly packed along tall spikes
Foliage:	Mounds of maplelike leaves with smaller leaves climbing the tall stems
Bloom length:	4 weeks, with a repeat in September
Height:	3–6 feet **Width/spacing:** 24 inches
Light:	Sun to light shade **Soil:** Rich, moist, well-drained
Care:	Stake as needed; watch for slugs; mulch for winter
Uses:	Architectural accent, blue garden, cottage garden, background
Propagation:	Seed
Problems:	Often needs staking; likes cool evenings
Insider's tips:	The delphinium pictured is a Duncan McLashen cross from England. His new plants are shorter, stockier and longer-lived. Look for more English hybrids called New Millennium Delphiniums from Dowdeswell Delphiniums in New Zealand.
Combines with:	*Monarda didyma* 'Gardenview Scarlet', *Rosa* 'Betty Prior', *Echinacea purpurea* 'White Swan', *Heliopsis helianthoides* 'Summer Sun', *Helictotrichon sempervirens*, *Eupatorium maculatum* 'Gateway'

Delphinium grandiflorum 'Blue Butterfly'
BLUE BUTTERFLY DWARF CHINESE DELPHINIUM

Plant type:	Biennial **Zone:** 3–7
Flower:	Gentian blue, open-faced flowers along multiple stems form loose spikes
Foliage:	Mounds of delicately incised maplelike leaves
Bloom length:	6 weeks, not including repeat
Height:	12–18 inches **Width/spacing:** 12 inches
Light:	Sun to light shade **Soil:** Rich, moist, well-drained
Care:	Deadhead to prolong bloom
Uses:	Cottage garden, bright color accent, edger
Propagation:	Seed; often self-sows
Problems:	Short-lived; in my Zone 5 garden, this plant acts more like a biennial than a perennial.
Insider's tips:	Because the color is so spectacular, I try to make sure my plants self-sow, or I buy new ones as necessary. Beware, this color of blue does not go well with the violet-blue of campanulas.
Combines with:	*Coreopsis verticillata* 'Moonbeam', *Dianthus* x *allwoodii* 'Doris', *Iris pallida* 'Argentea-variegata', *Heuchera* 'Plum Pudding'

Leucanthemum (Chrysanthemum) x *superbum* 'Ryan's White'

RYAN'S WHITE SHASTA DAISY

Plant type:	Perennial **Zone:** 4–9
Flower:	Typical Shasta—2 inches across with white petals and yellow center
Foliage:	Glossy, dark green, along sturdy stems from a basal mound
Bloom length:	10-plus weeks
Height:	24–30 inches **Width/spacing:** 24 inches
Light:	Full sun **Soil:** Average, well-drained
Care:	Deadhead for repeat bloom
Uses:	Long bloomer, cottage garden, daisy garden, mid-border, cut flower
Propagation:	Division in spring or fall; replace as necessary
Problems:	May frost-heave in winter
Insider's tips:	In 1999, 'Ryan's White' proved to be outstanding in its first year in the Chicago Botanic Garden plant evaluation trials. Even without regular deadheading, it outbloomed others and looked consistently upright!
Combines with:	*Veronica spicata* 'Blue Charm', *Lychnis chalcedonica*, *Delphinium grandiflorum* 'Blue Butterfly', *Hemerocallis* 'Happy Returns', *Rosa* 'Showbiz'

JUNE–SEPTEMBER

Phlox x *arendsii* 'Spring Pearl' Series
SPRING PEARL BORDER PHLOX, GARDEN PHLOX

Plant type:	Perennial **Zone:** 3–8
Foliage:	Upright leafy stems
Flower:	Fragrant clusters of florets with red eye form a larger bloom head
Bloom length:	10 week, September reblooms are smaller
Height:	18–24 inches **Width/spacing:** 18 inches
Light:	Sun to light shade **Soil:** Rich, moist, well-drained
Care:	Deadhead to encourage continued bloom; does not need staking
Uses:	Cottage garden, cut flower, showy color in the border, fragrance
Propagation:	Division of offshoots after three years
Problems:	Has good mildew resistance, relative to the garden it's grown in!
Insider's tips:	DeVroomen Holland Garden Products introduced this group of phlox. Each "Miss" is a different color with a darker eye zone: 'Miss Jill', white; 'Miss Jo-Ellen', white-tinged pink; 'Miss Karen', dark rose; 'Miss Margie', lilac-blue; 'Miss Mary', clear red; and 'Miss Wilma', pale lilac.
Combines with:	*Perovskia atriplicifolia, Helictotrichon sempervirens, Rosa* 'Knock Out', *Liatris spicata* 'Kobold', *Platycodon grandiflorus* 'Mariesii'

157

Salvia x *superba* 'Blue Hill'
BLUE HILL SALVIA, MEADOW SAGE

Plant type:	Perennial **Zone:** 4–9
Flower:	Deep violet-blue flowers form spike
Foliage:	Upright, aromatic
Bloom length:	10 weeks; repeat bloom
Height:	12–15 inches **Width/spacing:** 12 inches
Light:	Full sun **Soil:** Average, well-drained
Care:	Deadhead for repeat bloom
Uses:	Showy color in the border, blue garden, herb garden, attracts butterflies
Propagation:	Division in spring or fall
Problems:	Cut back if gets floppy
Insider's tips:	This is one of the bluest of the perennial salvias. Even with its short stature, it usually "lodges" or falls apart at the center and must be cut back to maintain compactness.
Combines with:	*Callirhoe involucrata, Geranium endressii* 'Wargrave Pink', *Phlox paniculata* 'Spring Pearl Series', *Leucanthemum* x *superbum* 'Snowcap'

Salvia verticillata 'Purple Rain'
PURPLE RAIN WHORLED SALVIA

Plant type:	Perennial, drought-tolerant **Zone:** 4–7
Flower:	Lilac-purple whorls form loose spike
Foliage:	Mounded medium green almost heart-shaped leaves
Bloom length:	6 weeks plus repeat bloom
Height:	24 inches **Width/spacing:** 24 inches
Light:	Full sun **Soil:** Average, well-drained
Care:	Deadhead for repeat bloom and neatness; needs to be done twice during summer
Uses:	Herb garden, edger, filler, attracts butterflies
Propagation:	Division in spring or fall
Problems:	Watch for slugs during wet summers
Insider's tips:	This new cultivar provides a different texture from the typical upright, spiked salvia.
Combines with:	*Echinacea purpurea* 'Crimson Star', *Leucanthemum* x *superbum* 'Snowcap', *Coreopsis grandiflora* 'Sunray', *Solidago* x 'Golden Baby', *Lychnis chalcedonica*

Veronica spicata 'Blue Charm'
BLUE CHARM SPIKED SPEEDWELL

Plant type:	Perennial **Zone:** 3–7
Flower:	Lavender-blue spikes
Foliage:	Glossy, pointed foliage along stems
Bloom length:	7–10 weeks, including repeat bloom
Height:	30–36 inches **Width/spacing:** 30 inches
Light:	Sun to light shade **Soil:** Average, well-drained
Care:	Cut back if it flops after initial bloom time
Uses:	Mid-border, spiky accent, cottage garden, long bloomer
Propagation:	Division in spring
Problems:	Black spot
Insider's tips:	I also like *Veronica longifolia* var. *subsessilis,* a 30-inch-tall speedwell with larger leaves; it's a gentle recliner, which is very hard to find in the trade.
Combines with:	*Monarda didyma* 'Gardenview Scarlet', *Coreopsis grandiflora* 'Sunray', *Leucanthemum* x *superbum* 'Ryan's White'

Coreopsis verticillata 'Moonbeam'
MOONBEAM THREADLEAF COREOPSIS

Plant type:	Perennial **Zone:** 3–9
Flower:	Soft yellow, 1-inch daisy on wiry stems
Foliage:	Extremely fine-textured, needlelike, fragrant
Bloom length:	15-plus weeks
Height:	18–24 inches **Width/spacing** 24 inches
Light:	Full sun **Soil:** Average, well-drained
Care:	Deadheading by giving it a "haircut" prolongs bloom time
Uses:	Long bloomer, textural softener, edger, attracts butterflies
Propagation:	Division in spring or fall
Problems:	Dies out if shaded by other garden plants or if soil is too soggy
Insider's tips:	1992's Perennial Plant of the Year combines well with most plants and is valuable for its long season of bloom. 'Golden Showers', another thread-leafed variety, needs restraining and regular division.
Combines with:	*Geranium wallichianum* 'Buxton's Variety', *Leucanthemum* x *superbum* 'Snowcap', *Veronica alpina* 'Goodness Grows', *Delphinium grandiflorum* 'Blue Butterfly', *Iris pallida* 'Argentea-variegata'

Gaura lindheimeri
GAURA, WHIRLING BUTTERFLIES

Plant type: Perennial, native, drought-tolerant   **Zone:** 5–8

Flower: Pink-tinged white; often described as small butterflies

Foliage: Willowlike leaves and long stems give loose, airy effect

Bloom length: 12 weeks

Height: 3–5 feet   **Width/spacing:** 30 inches

Light: Full sun to part shade in the South

Soil: Average to poor, well-drained

Care: Plan for some support of lax stems by planting behind a plant that can hold up stems

Uses: Mid-border, weaver, long bloomer, cottage garden

Propagation: Seed-sown in fall

Problems: Taproot does not like disturbance

Insider's tips: A Texas native, this lax-stemmed long bloomer needs support from neighboring plants—my favorite is a shrub, crimson barberry. Gaura begins blooming at about 2 feet, and the stems elongate up to 5 feet as bloom continues.

Combines with: *Caryopteris* x *clandonensis* 'Longwood Blue', *Pennisetum alopecuroides*, *Hemerocallis* 'Pink Lavender Appeal'

Gaura lindheimeri 'Siskiyou Pink'

SISKIYOU PINK GAURA

Plant type:	Perennial, drought-tolerant **Zone:** 5–8
Flower:	Small, rich pink butterflies
Foliage:	Willowlike leaves are tinged red on long stems; has a loose, airy effect
Bloom length:	12 weeks
Height:	2–3 feet **Width/spacing:** 24–30 inches
Light:	Full sun to part shade in the South
Soil:	Average to poor, well-drained
Care:	Easy
Uses:	Mid-border, weaver, long bloomer, cottage garden
Propagation:	May be patented, so do not propagate
Problems:	Not as floppy as parent
Insider's tips:	This more compact form does not require staking and has showier pink flowers.
Combines with:	*Perovskia atriplicifolia, Artemisia schmidtiana* 'Silver Mound', *Leucanthemum* x *superbum* 'Ryan's White', *Rosa* 'Flower Carpet White'

Hemerocallis 'Happy Returns'
HAPPY RETURNS DAYLILY

Plant type:	Perennial **Zone:** 3–9
Flower:	Lemon yellow lily opens in evening and remains for twenty-four hours
Foliage:	Straplike leaves form a neat, fountainlike mound
Bloom length:	18 weeks
Height:	18 inches **Width/spacing:** 24 inches
Light:	Full sun, light shade (lower light results in fewer blooms)
Soil:	Average, well-drained
Care:	Deadhead for neatness; cut back stems when all buds have bloomed; replenish soil annually
Uses:	Long bloomer, edger, mixed border, cut flower, container
Propagation:	Division every three years in spring or fall
Problems:	Needs fertilizing and division to reinvigorate clumps
Insider's tips:	Color blends easily with most garden plants. If the plant is no longer blooming profusely, it needs division, fresh nutrient-rich soil, and a little added fertilizer.
Combines with:	*Veronica* 'Sunny Border Blue', *Leucanthemum* x *superbum* 'Snowcap', *Salvia* x *superba* 'May Night', *Campanula carpatica* 'Deep Blue Clips', *Delphinium* x *belladonna* 'Bellamosa'

Hemerocallis 'Stella d'Oro'
STELLA D'ORO DAYLILY

Plant type:	Perennial **Zone:** 3–9
Flower:	Golden-yellow six-petaled lily
Foliage:	Straplike leaves form a neat, fountainlike mound
Bloom length:	18 weeks **Height:** 18–24 inches **Width/spacing:** 30 inches
Light:	Full sun, light shade (lower light results in fewer blooms)
Soil:	Rich, moist, well-drained
Care:	Deadhead for neatness; cut back stems when all buds have bloomed
Uses:	Long bloomer, edger, mixed border, cut flower, container, new American garden
Propagation:	Division every three years in spring or fall; replant in nutrient-enriched soil
Problems:	Needs fertilizing and division to reinvigorate clumps
Insider's tips:	This is the second-most overused perennial, and I am tired of seeing it in great swaths with black-eyed Susan, which is exactly the same color! Try the combinations below to stand apart from your neighbors.
Combines with:	*Iris sibirica*, *Phlox paniculata* 'David', *Arabis caucasica* 'Snowcap', *Salvia* x *superba* 'May Night', *Echinacea purpurea* 'White Swan'

Rosa 'Betty Prior'
BETTY PRIOR ROSE

Plant type:	Floribunda rose **Zone:** 4–9
Flower:	Rich rosy pink, five-petaled, single roses born in clusters; light fragrance
Foliage:	Semi-glossy, clean foliage, somewhat vase-shaped habit
Bloom length:	15 weeks
Height:	5 feet **Width/spacing:** 3 feet
Light:	Full sun **Soil:** Rich, moist, well-drained
Care:	Deadhead for neatness
Uses:	Cottage garden, long bloomer, mixed border, disease-resistant
Propagation:	A patented plant—do not propagate
Problems:	Occasional uneven growth
Insider's tips:	'Betty Prior' has been around for a long time and is still a carefree favorite. Make good use of its 5-foot height and its almost continuous bloom habit.
Combines with:	*Delphinium* x *elatum*, *Salvia* x *superba* 'May Night', *Helictotrichon sempervirens*, *Hemerocallis* 'Pink Lavender Appeal', *Artemisia ludoviciana* 'Valerie Finnis'

Rosa 'Carefree Delight'
CAREFREE DELIGHT ROSE

Plant type:	Shrub rose **Zone:** 4–9
Flower:	Many clusters of peachy pink singles; coral buds; light fragrance
Foliage:	Very shrubby with small glossy leaves and a good mounded form
Bloom length:	At least 15 weeks; it just keeps repeat blooming
Height:	30–36 inches **Width/spacing:** 5 feet
Light:	Full sun **Soil:** Rich, moist, well-drained
Care:	Hardly any; it performs well, even without deadheading
Uses:	Long bloomer, accent, cottage garden, mixed border, disease-resistant
Propagation:	A patented plant—do not propagate
Problems:	None
Insider's tips:	I passed this rose up the first time I saw it, thinking that the flower color was too peachy. After watching the consistent and profuse repeat bloom, I decided that creative combinations would easily overcome my prejudgment.
Combines with:	*Ajuga* 'Jungle Beauty', *Veronica spicata* 'Blue Charm', *Hemerocallis* 'Happy Returns', *Platycodon grandiflorus* 'Mariesii', *Campanula lactiflora*, *Perovskia atriplicifolia*

Rosa 'Carefree Wonder'
CAREFREE WONDER ROSE

Plant type:	Shrub rose **Zone:** 4–9
Flower:	Typical rose flower with rich pink face and creamy reverse
Foliage:	Glossy, green, not leggy (shrub rose)
Bloom length:	Unbelievable 12-plus weeks
Height:	3–4 feet **Width/spacing:** 3 feet
Light:	Full sun **Soil:** Average to rich, evenly moist
Care:	Easy; deadhead for repeat bloom
Uses:	Long bloom, accent, mixed border, rose garden, disease-resistant
Propagation:	A patented plant—do not propagate
Problems:	Occasional grasshoppers
Insider's tips:	I've grown this rose for ten years. I encourage repeat bloom with New Jersey green sand. (See rose care in chapter 11.)
Combines with:	*Helictotrichon sempervirens, Salvia* x *superba* 'May Night', *Campanula carpatica* 'Deep Blue Clips', *Hemerocallis* 'Ice Carnival', *Phlox paniculata* 'David'

Rosa 'Flower Carpet'
FLOWER CARPET ROSE

Plant type:	Shrub rose, groundcover **Zone:** 4–9
Flower:	This 2-inch rose flower is sometimes described as iridescent pink.
Foliage:	Glossy, smaller rose foliage
Bloom length:	15 weeks
Height:	18–24 inches **Width/spacing:** 24–30 inches
Light:	Sun to light shade **Soil:** Average to rich, evenly moist
Care:	Deadhead for neatness
Uses:	Groundcover, accent, border edger, mixed border, long bloomer, disease-resistant
Propagation:	A patented plant—do not propagate
Problems:	None
Insider's tips:	At first I thought that the hot pink blooms would be difficult in the garden, but it even works with the "hot" golden-yellow of *Oenothera fruticosa* ssp. *glauca*.
Combines with:	*Heuchera* 'Smokey Rose', *Oenothera fruticosa* ssp. *glauca*, *Platycodon grandiflorus* 'Sentimental Blue', *Artemisia stelleriana* 'Silver Brocade', x *Heucherella alba* 'Bridget Bloom'

Rosa 'Knock Out'
KNOCK OUT ROSE

Plant type:	Shrub rose **Zone:** 4–9
Flower:	Medium-sized clusters of deep, rosy red typical rose blooms
Foliage:	Glossy, dark green
Bloom length:	10–15 weeks
Height:	30–36 inches **Width/spacing:** 30 inches
Light:	Full sun **Soil:** Rich, moist, well-drained
Care:	Deadhead for neatness
Uses:	Groundcover, accent, rose garden, mixed border, long bloomer, disease-resistant
Propagation:	A patented plant—do not propagate
Problems:	None
Insider's tips:	This All-America Rose Selection for 2000 is brand new from William Radler of Boerner Botanic Garden, New Berlin, Wisconsin.
Combines with:	*Platycodon grandiflorus* 'Sentimental Blue', *Artemisia stelleriana* 'Silver Brocade', x *Heucherella alba* 'Bridget Bloom', *Veronica* 'Minuet', *Leucanthemum* x *superbum* 'Snowcap'

Rosa 'Showbiz'
SHOWBIZ ROSE

Plant type:	Floribunda rose **Zone:** 4–9
Flower:	Scarlet clusters of small perfect roses—like a bouquet
Foliage:	Glossy, dark green
Bloom length:	16 weeks
Height:	24–30 inches **Width/spacing:** 30–36 inches
Light:	Full sun **Soil:** Rich, moist, well-drained
Care:	Deadhead for neatness and repeat bloom
Uses:	Accent, rose garden, mixed border, long bloomer, disease-resistant
Propagation:	A patented plant—do not propagate
Problems:	None
Insider's tips:	The shorter stature of this rose demands that it be placed toward the front of the border. The red color has just a hint of yellow in it and should not be combined with "blue-pinks" like *Rosa* 'Flower Carpet'.
Combines with:	*Artemisia stelleriana* 'Silver Brocade', *Stachys byzantina* 'Silver Carpet', *Salvia* x *superba* 'Blue Hill', *Platycodon grandiflorus* 'Sentimental Blue', *Leucanthemum* x *superbum* 'Ryan's White'

Scabiosa columbaria 'Butterfly Blue'
BUTTERFLY BLUE PINCUSHION FLOWER

Plant type: Perennial   **Zone:** 3–9

Flower: Pale blue pincushion on a wiry stem; heavy bloomer

Foliage: Neat, compact, mat-forming

Bloom length: 18 weeks

Height: 15 inches   **Width/spacing:** 15 inches

Light: Sun to light shade   **Soil:** Average, well-drained, likes lime

Care: Deadhead for rebloom

Uses: Long bloomer, blue garden, edger, rock garden, cottage garden, attracts butterflies

Propagation: A patented perennial—do not propagate

Problems: Short-lived

Insider's tips: Although a very long bloomer, the pale flowers are not very showy in the garden. Plant in groups of at least three for best display.

Combines with: *Rosa* cultivars, *Stachys byzantina* 'Silver Carpet', *Coreopsis verticillata* 'Moonbeam', *Iris pallida* 'Argentea-variegata', *Hemerocallis* 'Happy Returns', *Callirhoe involucrata*, *Dianthus* x *allwoodii* 'Doris'

Veronica alpina 'Goodness Grows'
GOODNESS GROWS VERONICA, SPEEDWELL

Plant type:	Perennial **Zone:** 3–8
Flower:	Dark blue, spike
Foliage:	Low, mat-forming, shiny; evergreen in the South
Bloom length:	14-plus weeks
Height:	10–12 inches **Width/spacing:** 12 inches
Light:	Full sun **Soil:** Average, well-drained
Care:	Deadhead for neatness and more bloom
Uses:	Edger, long bloomer, disease-resistant, attracts butterflies
Propagation:	Division in spring or fall
Problems:	Lower light results in little bloom
Insider's tips:	Flowers start blooming early in the season and continue to bloom into October with or without deadheading. Plants will benefit from deadheading, as browned spikes detract from the blooms.
Combines with:	*Verbena canadensis* 'Homestead Purple', *Aster novae-angliae* 'Purple Dome', *Coreopsis verticillata* 'Moonbeam', *Iris pallida* 'Argentea-variegata', *Hemerocallis* 'Happy Returns', *Callirhoe involucrata*

CHAPTER 5

July

*The Fireworks of
Daylilies in the
Sun and Astilbes
in the Shade*

Aconitum x *cammarum* 'Newry Blue'
NEWRY BLUE MONKSHOOD

Plant type: Perennial   **Zone:** 3–7

Flower: Violet-blue, hooded blooms form a spike, similar to delphinium

Foliage: Glossy, maplelike leaves

Bloom length: 4–6 weeks   **Height:** 3–4 feet   **Width/spacing:** 24 inches

Light: Light shade; tolerates less sun in the South

Soil: Rich, moist, well-drained   **Care:** Does not need staking

Uses: Cut flower, in place of delphinium, cottage garden, earlier-blooming monkshood, architectural accent, showy color

Propagation: Division difficult due to brittle roots; rarely needs division; seed needs cold stratification

Problems: All plant parts are poisonous if eaten!

Insider's tips: This is one of the earliest-blooming monkshoods, and it's easier to grow than delphiniums. The even shorter, 2- to 3-foot 'Bressingham Spire' is very similar.

Combines with: *Phlox paniculata* 'David' or 'Eva Cullum', *Lychnis chalcedonica*, *Leucanthemum* x *superbum* 'Aglaia', *Hemerocallis* 'Tetrina's Daughter'

Artemisia ludoviciana 'Valerie Finnis'
VALERIE FINNIS WHITE SAGE

Plant type:	Perennial **Zone:** 4–9
Flower:	Branched, gray panicles
Foliage:	Silvery gray, nicely dissected leaves on upright stems
Bloom length:	8 weeks, plus a dried effect
Height:	15–18 inches **Width/spacing:** 18 inches
Light:	Full sun **Soil:** Average to poor, well-drained
Care:	Good drainage is mandatory.
Uses:	Herb garden, foliage color, mid-border, accent, container
Propagation:	Stem cuttings in early summer
Problems:	Can become floppy with too much rain
Insider's tips:	Use this artemisia in place of 'Silver King' and 'Silver Queen', which are invasive and run all over the garden!
Combines with:	*Hemerocallis* 'Ice Carnival', *Veronica* 'Sunny Border Blue', *Phlox paniculata* 'Eva Cullum', *Hemerocallis* 'Rocket City', *Sedum* x 'Autumn Joy', *Rosa* cultivars

Artemisia stelleriana 'Silver Brocade'
SILVER BROCADE BEACH WORMWOOD, PERENNIAL DUSTY MILLER

Plant type: Perennial **Zone:** 4–8

Flower: Yellow (does not add to value of foliage, so remove)

Foliage: Soft, deeply fingered silver, creeping; looks like a creeping dusty miller

Bloom length: N/A

Height: 6 inches **Width/spacing:** 18 inches

Light: Full sun **Soil:** Average to poor, well-drained

Care: Deadhead; cut back if too sprawling

Uses: Edger, foliage color, softener, accent, herb garden, container

Propagation: Stem cuttings in early summer

Problems: Rots with excessive moisture and humidity

Insider's tips: An introduction from the University of British Columbia Botanical Garden, this does best if planted along a stone or brick path laid in sand.

Combines with: *Coreopsis verticillata* 'Moonbeam', *Geranium sanguineum* var. *striatum*, *Aster* x *frikartii* 'Monch', *Rosa* 'Knock Out'

Astilbe x *arendsii* 'Bressingham Beauty'
BRESSINGHAM BEAUTY ASTILBE

Plant type:	Perennial **Zone:** 4–9
Flower:	Loose pink plume
Foliage:	Finely cut, dark green leaves form tall mounds
Bloom length:	3–5 weeks
Height:	36 inches **Width/spacing:** 30 inches
Light:	Part shade **Soil:** Rich, moist
Care:	Maintain moisture and fertility of the soil; does not need staking
Uses:	Back of the border, shade garden, woodland garden, architectural accent, easy care, wet garden
Propagation:	Division in spring
Problems:	None
Insider's tips:	'Bressingham Beauty' is one of the taller astilbes. Mixing astilbes of differing heights, flower colors, and bloom times makes for an interesting, easy-care shade garden.
Combines with:	*Cimicifuga racemosa, Tradescantia* x *andersoniana* 'Zwanenberg Blue', *Osmunda cinnamomea, Lobelia siphilitica*

Astilbe chinensis (*taquetii*) 'Superba'
LANCE ASTILBE, CHINESE ASTILBE

Plant type: Perennial   **Zone:** 4–8

Flower: Rosy-violet clusters form a lance shape

Foliage: Finely cut but rounded leaves form a substantial mound

Bloom length: 3–5 weeks

Height: 48 inches   **Width/spacing:** 24 inches

Light: Part shade   **Soil:** Rich, moist; tolerant of drier soils

Care: Maintain fertility of the soil

Uses: Back of the border, shade garden, woodland garden, architectural accent, easy care

Propagation: Division in spring or fall; I have yet to divide any of my astilbes.

Problems: None

Insider's tips: This astilbe may last into September and tolerates drought better than most. *Astilbe chinensis* 'Purpurkerze'—Purple Candle—is a richer color.

Combines with: *Liatris spicata* 'Kobold', *Asarum canadense, Onoclea sensibilis, Hosta* 'Piedmont Gold', *Thalictrum aquilegiifolium*

Astilbe japonica 'Red Sentinel'
RED SENTINEL JAPANESE ASTILBE

Plant type:	Perennial **Zone:** 4–8
Flower:	Light red, clustered plume
Foliage:	Finely cut, bronzed, dark green leaves in tight mounds
Bloom length:	2–4 weeks
Height:	28 inches **Width/spacing:** 24 inches
Light:	Part shade **Soil:** Rich, moist
Care:	Easy
Uses:	Woodland, water's edge, wet garden, cut flower
Propagation:	Division in spring; I have yet to divide any of my astilbes.
Problems:	Do not allow to dry out
Insider's tips:	July is the primary month of bloom for astilbes. By choosing other astilbes that bloom in June and August, you can create a succession of blooms throughout summer and even into September! See the astilbe flowering guide in appendix D.
Combines with:	*Hemerocallis* 'Ice Carnival', *Aconitum* x *cammarum* 'Newry Blue', *Hosta fluctuans* 'Sagae', *Lysimachia clethroides*

Astilbe simplicifolia 'Sprite'
STAR ASTILBE

Plant type:	Perennial **Zone:** 4–8
Flower:	Shell pink, arching sprays in a star shape
Foliage:	Fine-textured, glossy with bronze caste
Bloom length:	4–6 weeks
Height:	12 inches **Width/spacing:** 12 inches
Light:	Part shade **Soil:** Rich, moist
Care:	Maintain moisture and fertility of the soil
Uses:	Edger, woodland, water's edge, wet garden, cut flower
Propagation:	Division in spring
Problems:	Needs extra fertilizer and compost to renew supply of nutrients
Insider's tips:	Remember astilbes are "gross feeders," depleting soils of nutrients. Use compost with extra fertilizer to feed those roots.
Combines with:	*Heuchera* 'Plum Pudding', *Athyrium nipponicum* 'Pictum', *Asarum europaeum, Myosotis sylvatica*

Cimicifuga racemosa
SNAKEROOT, COHOSH

Plant type:	Perennial, native **Zone:** 3–7
Flower:	Many white "fluffs" forming a wandlike spike
Foliage:	Broad clumps with divided leaves, much like an elegant astilbe
Bloom length:	4–6 weeks
Height:	4–6 feet **Width/spacing:** 36 inches
Light:	Shade, part shade **Soil:** Rich, cool, moist; likes acid
Care:	Easy; leave seed heads
Uses:	Back of the border, naturalizes, shade garden, wildflower garden, architectural accent, attractive seedpods, attracts butterflies, wet garden
Propagation:	Division—this plant has a long taproot, so it doesn't divide easily
Problems:	Must have moist soil
Insider's tips:	Mix this with *Cimicifuga simplex* 'White Pearl' (3 feet tall, September–October bloom time) for extended bloom.
Combines with:	*Hosta fluctuans* 'Sagae', *Lobelia siphilitica*, *Lobelia cardinalis*, *Onoclea sensibilis*, *Ligularia stenocephala* 'The Rocket'

Eryngium yuccifolium
RATTLESNAKE MASTER

Plant type:	Perennial, native **Zone:** 4–9
Flower:	Creamy green, spiked balls
Foliage:	Stiff, narrow and branching; yucca-like
Bloom length:	4–6 weeks
Height:	30–36 inches **Width/spacing:** 24 inches
Light:	Full sun **Soil:** Average, well-drained
Care:	Easy
Uses:	Dried flower, mid-border, architectural accent, prairie/meadow, winter interest
Propagation:	Seed
Problems:	Bristly leaf margins
Insider's tips:	Here's a really unusual prairie native being brought into the garden as an accent. It's thought to be a cure for rattlesnake bite, but this seems unlikely. Children love the common name!
Combines with:	*Liatris spicata* 'Kobold', *Echinacea purpurea* 'Magnus' or 'White Swan', *Sporobolus heterolepsis*, *Asclepias tuberosa*

Filipendula rubra
QUEEN-OF-THE-PRAIRIE

Plant type:	Perennial, native **Zone:** 3–9
Flower:	Pink to peach panicles
Foliage:	Somewhat like a giant astilbe
Bloom length:	4–5 weeks
Height:	5–7 feet **Width/spacing:** 3 feet
Light:	Sun to light shade **Soil:** Rich, moist
Care:	Do not allow to dry out
Uses:	Back of the border, cottage garden, prairie/meadow, architectural accent
Propagation:	Division in fall
Problems:	If foliage becomes tattered, cut back to rejuvenate.
Insider's tips:	The cultivar 'Venusta' has deeper pink to rose flowers.
Combines with:	*Rosa* 'Carefree Delight', *Artemisia ludoviciana* 'Valerie Finnis', *Monarda didyma* 'Marshall's Delight', *Phlox paniculata* 'David', *Miscanthus sinensis* 'Malepartus'

Filipendula ulmaria 'Aurea'
QUEEN-OF-THE-MEADOW

Plant type:	Perennial, herb **Zone:** 2–9
Flower:	Scented sprays of white or cream
Foliage:	Mounds of yellow-green elmlike foliage that can be used as a sweetener
Bloom length:	5 weeks **Height:** 24 inches **Width/spacing:** 30 inches
Light:	Part shade to sun; sometimes scorches in afternoon sun
Soil:	Rich, moist, well-drained
Care:	Deadhead and cut back for foliage rejuvenation
Uses:	Mid-border, cottage garden, foliage color, herb garden, prairie/meadow
Propagation:	Division in spring or fall
Problems:	Dwindles in too much shade; seedlings revert to green foliage
Insider's tips:	The plant may lose some of its foliage coloration during bloom. Cut down after blooming for fresh late-season foliage growth and renewed yellow-green color.
Combines with:	Iris foliage, *Digitalis grandiflora, Corydalis lutea, Phlox paniculata* 'Fairest One', *Campanula poscharskyana, Salvia* x *superba* 'Blue Hill'

Hemerocallis 'Rocket City'

ROCKET CITY DAYLILY

Plant type:	Perennial **Zone:** 3–9
Flower:	Day-Glo orange, six-petaled lily with a cinnamon-sparkled center
Foliage:	Straplike leaves forming a neat, fountainlike mound
Bloom length:	6–7 weeks
Height:	30–34 inches **Width/spacing:** 36 inches
Light:	Sun to light shade **Soil:** Average, well-drained
Care:	Deadhead daily
Uses:	Cottage garden, mixed border, cut flower, daylily border
Propagation:	Division every three years in spring or fall
Problems:	Earwigs
Insider's tips:	This is one of the best orange daylilies! Experienced gardeners use orange to "punch up" the color palette.
Combines with:	*Hibiscus moscheutos* (white), *Artemisia ludoviciana* 'Valerie Finnis', *Salvia* x *superba* 'May Night' or 'Blue Hill', *Echinacea purpurea* 'White Swan', *Lilium* x 'Casablanca'

Hemerocallis 'Summer Wine'
SUMMER WINE DAYLILY

Plant type:	Perennial **Zone:** 3–9
Flower:	Rosy-wine, six-petaled lily with a yellow throat
Foliage:	Straplike leaves form a neat fountainlike mound
Bloom length:	6 weeks
Height:	24 inches **Width/spacing:** 24–30 inches
Light:	Sun to light shade **Soil:** Average, well-drained
Care:	Deadhead daily
Uses:	Mixed border, cut flower, accent color, cottage garden
Propagation:	Division every three years in spring or fall
Problems:	Earwigs
Insider's tips:	'Summer Wine' has an unusual flower color, as well as being a nice compact grower. See appendix E for more daylilies.
Combines with:	*Sedum* x 'Rosy Glow', *Nepeta mussinii* 'Blue Wonder', *Veronica* 'Minuet', *Rosa* 'Carefree Delight', *Echinacea purpurea* 'White Swan'

Hosta fluctuans 'Sagae' ('Variegata')
SAGAE VARIEGATED HOSTA

Plant type:	Perennial **Zone:** 3–9
Flower:	Loose clusters of pale lavender trumpets on 5-foot scapes!
Foliage:	Vase-shaped plant with large blue-green leaves with creamy yellow edges
Bloom length:	4 weeks
Height:	28–30 inches **Width/spacing:** 4–5 feet
Light:	Open shade **Soil:** Rich, moist, well-drained
Care:	Fall clean up
Uses:	Specimen, massed, mixed hosta border, shade garden, cut flower
Propagation:	Division in spring when plants are a mature size
Problems:	Some deer-browse
Insider's tips:	Hosta of the Year in 2000! In five years, mine have not grown to four feet wide, perhaps due to root-competition from a Norway maple.
Combines with:	*Thalictrum aquilegiifolium* 'Album', *Hesperis matronalis*, *Brunnera macrophylla*, *Helleborus orientalis*, *Hosta* 'Halcyon'

Hosta 'Piedmont Gold'

PIEDMONT GOLD HOSTA

Plant type:	Perennial **Zone:** 3–9
Flower:	Densely clustered white lilies on rather short stems, showing just above the foliage mound
Foliage:	Chartreuse to yellow huge rounded leaves form a large mound
Bloom length:	4–5 weeks
Height:	28–30 inches **Width/spacing:** 3–4 feet
Light:	Part shade; tolerates morning sun
Soil:	Average, well-drained to moist
Care:	Easy
Uses:	Slug-resistant, bright foliage in shade, specimen, massed, mixed hosta border
Propagation:	Division in spring
Problems:	Deer-browse; sometimes slugs
Insider's tips:	Chartreuse to yellow foliage stands out in shaded gardens! 'Piedmont Gold' as a specimen planting becomes a beacon.
Combines with:	*Tradescantia* x *andersoniana* 'Zwanenberg Blue', *Aruncus dioicus*, *Astilbe* x *arendsii* 'Bressingham Beauty', *Polygonatum odoratum* 'Variegatum', *Digitalis grandiflora*, *Galium odoratum*

Hosta 'Sum and Substance'
SUM AND SUBSTANCE PLANTAIN LILY

Plant type:	Perennial **Zone:** 3–9
Flower:	White, tubular, clustered along short stems
Foliage:	Huge, shiny, chartreuse foliage of heavy substance
Bloom length:	6–8 weeks
Height:	3 feet **Width/spacing:** 5 feet
Light:	Part shade; morning sun turns foliage more yellow
Soil:	Average, well-drained to moist
Care:	Easy; foliage is slug resistant
Uses:	Specimen, massed, mixed hosta border, shade garden, cut flower
Propagation:	Division in early spring after five years
Problems:	Deer-browse; slow to reach mature width
Insider's tips:	All you need is one 'Sum and Substance' to be a show-stopper! Consider the space it will take up at maturity, because perennials planted too close will be eventually shaded out. Use annuals in the first few years around this hosta to fill in empty space.
Combines with:	*Aruncus dioicus, Astilbe simplicifolia* 'Praecox Alba', *Polygonatum odoratum* 'Variegatum', *Digitalis grandiflora, Hosta fortunei* 'Aureo-marginata'

Leucanthemum (*Chrysanthemum*) x *superbum* 'Aglaia'
AGLAIA DOUBLE SHASTA DAISY

Plant type:	Perennial **Zone:** 4–9
Flower:	White, fringed or double daisy; looks more like a chrysanthemum
Foliage:	Glossy, dark green, along sturdy (non-floppy) stems from a basal mound
Bloom length:	8 weeks **Height:** 2 feet **Width/spacing:** 18–24 inches
Light:	Full sun **Soil:** Average, well-drained
Care:	Deadhead to leaf axils for repeat bloom
Uses:	Cottage garden, daisy garden, mid-border, cut flower
Propagation:	Division in spring or fall; replace as necessary
Problems:	Short-lived; sometimes slugs
Insider's tips:	In the North, many Shasta daisies do not winter over due to frost heave. Firm the soil around its roots when applying a winter mulch or be prepared to replace the plant in the spring. Cultivar 'Esther Reed' is another 2-foot double with an even longer bloom time.
Combines with:	*Platycodon grandiflorus* 'Mariesii', *Monarda didyma* 'Marshall's Delight', *Lilium* x *'Stargazer'*, *Asclepias tuberosa*, *Hemerocallis* 'Summer Wine'

Liatris spicata 'Kobold'
KOBOLD GAY FEATHER, BLAZING STAR

Plant type:	Perennial **Zone:** 3–9
Flower:	Bright magenta spire; flowers from the top down
Foliage:	Mound of straplike leaves from which stems grow; stems have linear leaves
Bloom length:	4–6 weeks **Height:** 24–30 inches **Width/spacing:** 24 inches
Light:	Sun to light shade **Soil:** Average to rich, evenly moist
Care:	Cut back stems after blooming to improve appearance
Uses:	Mixed border, prairie/meadow, attracts butterflies, cut flower, dried flower, strong vertical effect
Propagation:	See Allan Armitage's book *Herbaceous Perennial Plants* for best propagation instructions.
Problems:	Stems flop and become an unsightly brown after blooming
Insider's tips:	For best display, be prepared to cut back browning stems right away. Unfortunately, this does not encourage a rebloom.
Combines with:	*Hemerocallis* 'Hyperion', *Rudbeckia fulgida* var. *sullivantii* 'Goldsturm', *Perovskia atriplicifolia*, *Echinacea purpurea*, *Monarda didyma* 'Raspberry Wine'

Ligularia stenocephala 'The Rocket'
THE ROCKET SPIKED LIGULARIA

Plant type: Perennial   **Zone:** 5–8

Flower: Spikes of bright yellow 18 to 24 inches long

Foliage: Mounds of large, heart-shaped to triangular leaves with dark purple stems

Bloom length: 4–6 weeks   **Height:** 4–5 feet   **Width/spacing:** 3 feet

Light: Part shade; must have afternoon shade

Soil: Average to rich, evenly moist

Care: Do not allow to dry out; deadhead for neatness

Uses: Strong vertical accent, back of the border, wet garden, shade garden, cottage garden

Propagation: Division in spring, but you must keep new plants constantly moist

Problems: Wilts easily

Insider's tips: Many gardeners give up on this plant because of the watering involved to keep it going. It also does better in summers with cooler evenings.

Combines with: *Monarda didyma* 'Gardenview Scarlet', *Lysimachia clethroides, Kalimeris pinnatifida, Lobelia siphilitica, Hosta* 'Piedmont Gold'

Lilium x 'Casablanca'
CASABLANCA ORIENTAL LILY

Plant type: Bulb   **Zone:** 4–8

Flower: White, outward-facing, very fragrant

Foliage: Dark green, straplike and pointed leaves becoming shorter as they climb the stems

Bloom length: 4 weeks, dependent on the number of buds produced

Height: 36–40 inches   **Width/spacing:** 12 inches

Light: Sun to light shade

Soil: Average, well-drained

Care: Deadhead for neatness

Uses: Offsets bright colors, accent, cut flower, fragrance, cottage garden, mid-border

Propagation: Buy new bulbs

Problems: Rabbits nip off the buds (and often don't even eat them!); may need staking

Insider's tips: I interplant lilies in groups of three throughout the perennial garden. Think of them as "exclamation marks"!

Combines with: *Hemerocallis* 'Rocket City', *Echinacea purpurea* 'Magnus', *Perovskia atriplicifolia*, *Hibiscus moscheutos* 'Lord Baltimore'

Lilium x 'Stargazer'
STARGAZER ORIENTAL LILY

Plant type: Bulb **Zone:** 4–8

Flower: Rich crimson-pink, darker-spotted, white-edged, upward-facing, fragrant

Foliage: Strong stems with glossy, straplike leaves

Bloom length: 4 weeks **Height:** 24 inches **Width/spacing:** 18 inches

Light: Full sun **Soil:** Average, well-drained

Care: Well-drained soil a must; bulbs rot in wet soils

Uses: Interplant in border, showy, cottage garden, fragrance, pot garden, cut flower

Propagation: Division

Problems: Rot; rabbits eat the buds just before opening!

Insider's tips: 'Stargazer' has been very popular as a pot plant sold in local grocery stores. It is equally impressive in the garden, needing little or no staking.

Combines with: *Echinacea purpurea* 'Magnus', *Phlox paniculata* 'David', *Aster* x *frikartii* 'Monch', *Kalimeris pinnatifida*, *Euphorbia corollata*, *Platycodon grandiflorus* 'Mariesii'

Lysimachia clethroides
GOOSENECK LOOSESTRIFE

Plant type:	Perennial **Zone:** 3–8
Flower:	White, curved, tapering, spike (like a goose's neck)
Foliage:	Upright, red stems; russet fall color
Bloom length:	4–5 weeks
Height:	30 inches **Width/spacing:** 3 feet
Light:	Sun to part shade **Soil:** Rich, moist, well-drained
Care:	Contain
Uses:	Wildflower, cottage garden, unusual flower form, architectural accent, fall color
Propagation:	Division anytime
Problems:	Aggressive spreader
Insider's tips:	Only use this plant next to plants that can compete with its aggressive behavior.
Combines with:	*Rudbeckia fulgida* var. *sullivantii* 'Goldsturm', *Echinacea purpurea* 'Magnus', *Hemerocallis* 'Rocket City', *Monarda didyma* 'Gardenview Scarlet', *Sporobolus heterolepis*

Origanum vulgare 'Aureum'
GOLDEN OREGANO

Plant type:	Perennial, herb **Zone:** 5–9
Flower:	Small, loose lavender panicles (flowers detract from the foliage)
Foliage:	Mat-forming clumps of oval chartreuse or yellow-green leaves; somewhat evergreen
Bloom length:	3–4 weeks
Height:	3 inches **Width/spacing:** 12 inches
Light:	Full sun **Soil:** Average, well-drained
Care:	Cut off flowers in bud
Uses:	Herb garden, cottage garden, edger, foliage color accent
Propagation:	Division in spring or fall
Problems:	Looses its good foliage color after blooming
Insider's tips:	Herbs in the perennial garden add interesting foliage contrasts, and they deter deer and rabbits from grazing.
Combines with:	*Nepeta mussinii* 'Blue Wonder', *Salvia* x *superba* 'Blue Hill', *Campanula carpatica* 'Deep Blue Clips', *Dianthus* x *allwoodii* 'Doris'

Platycodon grandiflorus 'Mariesii'
MARIESII BALLOON FLOWER

Plant type:	Perennial **Zone:** 3–8
Flower:	Balloonlike buds become violet-blue, star-shaped cups
Foliage:	Slender blue-green stems with oval leaves provide yellow fall color; often needs staking
Bloom length:	6–8 weeks **Height:** 24–30 inches **Width/spacing:** 18 inches
Light:	Sun to part shade **Soil:** Average, well-drained—even sandy
Care:	Pinch back by half in early June to avoid staking
Uses:	Mixed border, blue garden
Propagation:	Does not move easily; seed
Problems:	Late to emerge in spring, so be careful not to weed out; often needs support
Insider's tips:	The species is taller and floppier and often mixed up at the nursery. Try using the bottom ring of a tomato hoop (shorten with wire cutters) as a support for toppling plants. If left over winter, the hoop will serve as a marker for this slowly emerging plant in the spring. A children's favorite because of its balloon shape!
Combines with:	*Leucanthemum* x *superbum* 'Snowcap', *Phlox paniculata* 'Fairest One', *Lilium* x 'Stargazer', *Euphorbia corollata*

Platycodon grandiflorus 'Sentimental Blue'
SENTIMENTAL BLUE DWARF BALLOON FLOWER

Plant type: Perennial **Zone:** 3–8

Flower: Blue-violet balloons open with 2-inch wide cupped or belled flower

Foliage: Mounded ovals of blue-green

Bloom length: 8–10 weeks

Height: 8 inches **Width/spacing:** 10 inches

Light: Sun to part shade **Soil:** Average to rich, evenly moist

Care: Deadhead for neatness

Uses: Edger, prolific bloomer, unusual flower, cottage garden

Propagation: Division very difficult; seed

Problems: Late to emerge in spring, so be careful to not dig it up.

Insider's tips: A prolific bloomer with a tolerance for partial shade, preferably in the afternoon. Deadheads look like wet, dirty hankies and detract from the profuse bloom!

Combines with: *Iris pallida* 'Argentea-variegata', *Hemerocallis* 'Happy Returns', *Geranium sanguineum* var. *striatum, Heuchera* 'Plum Pudding', *Coreopsis verticillata* 'Moonbeam'

Sedum x 'Ruby Glow'
RUBY GLOW STONECROP

Plant type:	Perennial **Zone:** 3–9
Flower:	Dusky rose globular clusters
Foliage:	Purple-tinged, rounded leaves are somewhat succulent
Bloom length:	4–6 weeks
Height:	6–9 inches **Width/spacing:** 12 inches
Light:	Full sun **Soil:** Average to poor, well-drained
Care:	Easy
Uses:	Foliage color, edger, rock garden, cottage garden
Propagation:	Stem cuttings in early summer
Problems:	Any shade will cause foliage to become green; overly moist soils can cause rotting of succulent foliage
Insider's tips:	Cultivar 'Vera Jameson' is an improved seedling of 'Ruby Glow'. I also like 'Bertram Anderson' for its similar coloring but with a stronger branching pattern (though it's hard to find).
Combines with:	*Veronica alpina* 'Goodness Grows', *Scabiosa columbaria* 'Butterfly Blue', *Helictotrichon sempervirens, Allium senescens* 'Glaucum'

Silphium perfoliatum
CUP PLANT

Plant type: Perennial, native   **Zone:** 2–8

Flower: Yellow daisies in loose clusters at the top of a very tall plant

Foliage: Large opposite leaves form a cup around the stem

Bloom length: 6–8 weeks

Height: 5–8 feet   **Width/spacing:** 30–36 inches

Light: Sun to light shade   **Soil:** Average to poor, well-drained

Care: Easy; do not fertilize, as this encourages floppy, weak stems

Uses: Attracts birds, architectural accent, prairie/meadow, background

Propagation: Self-sows moderately

Problems: Too tall for many gardens

Insider's tips: This prairie native has recently become a popular "designer" plant. And children will love to watch birds visit the "cups" when filled with rainwater!

Combines with: *Sorghastrum nutans* 'Sioux Blue', *Sporobolus heterolepsis*, *Hibiscus moscheutos* 'Lord Baltimore', *Boltonia asteroides*, *Perovskia atriplicifolia*

Solidago x 'Golden Baby'
GOLDEN BABY GOLDENROD

Plant type: Perennial   **Zone:** 3–9

Flower: Small, bright yellow flowers form plumed head

Foliage: Tall, upright stems with lancelike leaves

Bloom length: 4–6 weeks

Height: 2–3 feet   **Width/spacing:** 12 inches

Light: Sun to light shade   **Soil:** Average, well-drained

Care: Needs division to curb spread, either in spring or fall

Uses: Prairie/meadow, mid-border, cottage garden, attracts butterflies

Propagation: Division in spring

Problems: Powdery mildew

Insider's tips: Other interesting goldenrods are *Solidago sphacelata* 'Golden Fleece' or *Solidago caesia* for partial shade. You may need to stake the taller goldenrods.

Combines with: *Perovskia atriplicifolia, Liatris spicata* 'Kobold', *Echinacea purpurea* 'White Swan', *Euphorbia corollata*

Stokesia laevis
STOKES ASTER

Plant type:	Perennial, native **Zone:** 5–9
Flower:	Lavender-blue, 3-inch ragged daisy with white center
Foliage:	Pointed, dark green, shiny, straplike leaves; evergreen in the South
Bloom length:	4–6 weeks
Height:	12–24 inches **Width/spacing:** 18 inches
Light:	Sun to light shade **Soil:** Average, well-drained
Care:	Deadhead to lateral buds, then to basal foliage, which is often evergreen through winter
Uses:	Wildflower, mid-border, cut flower, attracts butterflies
Propagation:	Division in spring every four years to regenerate plant
Problems:	Rots where winters are wet
Insider's tips:	The lavender-blue color is very showy, as is the shaggy daisy form. Cultivar 'Klaus Jelitto' has an even bigger flower!
Combines with:	*Artemisia ludoviciana* 'Valerie Finnis', *Coreopsis verticillata* 'Moonbeam', *Stachys officinalis* 'Alba', *Hemerocallis* 'Happy Returns', *Lychnis chalcedonica*

Alcea rosea
HOLLYHOCK

Plant type: Biennial **Zone:** 3–7

Flower: Many large, outward-facing, coral-rose cups along tall stems

Foliage: Rough, large, rounded leaves become smaller up the tall stems

Bloom length: 6–8 weeks **Height:** 6 feet **Width/spacing:** 18 inches

Light: Full sun **Soil:** Average, well-drained

Care: Treat rust with fungicidal soap and remove affected leaves; replace if problem persists

Uses: Cottage garden, back of the border, architectural accent

Propagation: Seed-sown just after the last frost in spring

Problems: Watch for spider mites, Japanese beetles, and occasionally rust; sometimes needs staking

Insider's tips: Treat as a biennial, although I have seen some that have "perennialized." A new *Alcea* 'Perennial Singles' from White Flower Farm is said to be perennial.

Combines with: *Delphinium* x *elatum, Miscanthus sinensis* 'Kaskade', *Buddleia davidii* 'Royal Red', *Aconitum napellus, Caryopteris* x *clandonensis*

Aster x *frikartii* 'Monch'
THE MONK FRIKART ASTER

Plant type:	Perennial **Zone:** 5–8
Flower:	Lavender-blue daisy with light yellow center
Foliage:	Basal leaves in clumps; multi-branched, almost shrublike
Bloom length:	8–12 weeks
Height:	2–3 feet **Width/spacing:** 2–3 feet
Light:	Full sun **Soil:** Average, well-drained
Care:	Benefits from pinching back, like mums; a light winter mulch helps in Zone 5
Uses:	Mid-border, long bloomer, blue garden, cottage garden, attracts butterflies
Propagation:	Division in spring; discard woody center (seedlings have varying color)
Problems:	May flop—needs support or earlier cutback
Insider's tips:	A Graham Stuart Thomas favorite, which he claims does not flop (one of the differences in English gardening?). This is not reliably winter-hardy in Zone 5! Adding a light winter mulch and leaving the plant up over winter may increase the rate of success.
Combines with:	*Hemerocallis* 'Stella d'Oro', *Hemerocallis* 'Summer Wine', *Phlox paniculata* 'Spring Pearl Series', *Malva alcea* 'Fastigiata', *Callirhoe involucrata*

Buddleia davidii 'Royal Red'
ROYAL RED BUTTERFLY BUSH

Plant type:	Perennial, shrublike **Zone:** 5–9
Flower:	Purple-red tubular flowers forming arching spikes, fragrant
Foliage:	Gray-green, willowlike leaves on arching woody stems; a dieback shrub in the North
Bloom length:	15 weeks
Height:	5 feet **Width/spacing:** 4–5 feet
Light:	Full sun **Soil:** Average to rich, evenly moist
Care:	Cut back to live wood in the spring
Uses:	Attracts butterflies, long bloomer, fragrance, back of the border, architectural accent
Propagation:	Stem cuttings taken in early summer
Problems:	May not overwinter; dies in extremely cold winters with no snow cover
Insider's tips:	To assure overwintering in the North, try mounding with compost after the ground is frozen. *Buddleia* 'Black Knight' and 'Pink Profusion' are shorter cultivars and have silvery foliage.
Combines with:	*Rudbeckia nitida* 'Herbstsonne', *Geranium* x *magnificum*, *Echinacea purpurea* 'White Swan', *Asclepias tuberosa*, *Eupatorium maculatum* 'Gateway'

Campanula carpatica 'Deep Blue Clips'
DEEP BLUE CLIPS CARPATHIAN BELLFLOWER, TUSSOCK HAREBELL

Plant type: Perennial **Zone:** 3–7

Flower: Dark violet-blue, wide, upturned bell

Foliage: Low mound of small, heart-shaped, dense leaves

Bloom length: 6–8 weeks

Height: 8 inches **Width/spacing:** 12 inches

Light: Part sun; likes some shade in heat of the day

Soil: Average, well-drained

Care: Easy; deadhead for repeat bloom

Uses: Edger, mixed border, massing, rock garden, small space

Propagation: Division in spring—not easily done because of brittle roots

Problems: Slugs (use diatomaceous earth)

Insider's tips: This darker colored 'Blue Clips' is new. Both plants have good repeat bloom if kept deadheaded and benefit from cutting back if they become straggly in late summer.

Combines with: *Dianthus* x *allwoodii* 'Doris', *Arabis caucasica* 'Snowcap', *Helictotrichon sempervirens*, *Coreopsis verticillata* 'Moonbeam', *Iris pallida* 'Argentea-variegata'

Echinacea purpurea 'Magnus'
MAGNUS PURPLE CONEFLOWER

Plant type: Perennial, drought-tolerant   **Zone:** 3–8

Flower: Rich rose daisy with orange-brown central cone

Foliage: Course, hairy leaves from a basal mound

Bloom length: 8 weeks

Height: 24–30 inches   **Width/spacing:** 2–3 feet

Light: Sun to part shade   **Soil:** Average, well-drained; tolerates dryness

Care: Easy; leave seed heads to feed the birds in winter

Uses: Mid-border, prairie/meadow, woodland edge, naturalizes, cut flower, leave seed heads for winter interest, attracts butterflies

Propagation: Division in spring

Problems: Seedlings not likely to come true, having cross-pollinated with other coneflowers nearby; rogue out unwanted seedlings in spring

Insider's tips: Selected cultivars like 'Magnus' have better color than the species, which is a 'muddy' mauve.

Combines with: *Liatris spicata* 'Kobold', *Hemerocallis* 'Hyperion', *Monarda didyma* 'Raspberry Wine', *Veronica* 'Sunny Border Blue', *Perovskia atriplicifolia*

Echinacea purpurea 'White Swan'
WHITE SWAN CONEFLOWER

Plant type:	Perennial, drought-tolerant **Zone:** 3–9
Flower:	Large white daisies with bronze-orange cone
Foliage:	Course, hairy leaves from a basal mound
Bloom length:	8–10 weeks
Height:	30–36 inches **Width/spacing:** 30 inches
Light:	Sun to light shade **Soil:** Average, well-drained
Care:	Deadhead for repeat bloom, leaving late seed heads for the winter birds
Uses:	Mid-border, prairie/meadow, woodland edge, naturalizes, cut flower, leave seed heads for winter interest, attracts butterflies
Propagation:	Division in spring
Problems:	Seedlings may not come true
Insider's tips:	This coneflower is showier in combinations and continues the "daisy season" with the Shastas.
Combines with:	*Hemerocallis* 'Rocket City', *Delphinium grandiflorum* 'Blue Butterfly', *Asclepias tuberosa, Salvia* x *superba* 'May Night', *Buddleia davidii* 'Royal Red', *Verbena canadensis* 'Homestead Purple'

Eupatorium maculatum 'Gateway'
GATEWAY SPOTTED JOE-PYE WEED

Plant type:	Perennial **Zone:** 4–8
Flower:	Numerous small, rosy-purple flowers form a huge 12-inch dome
Foliage:	Stately, whorled leaves with purple stems
Bloom length:	6–8 weeks
Height:	5 feet **Width/spacing:** 3 feet
Light:	Full sun **Soil:** Rich, moist, well-drained
Care:	Easy
Uses:	Prairie/meadow, back of the border, attracts butterflies, dried flower, architectural accent
Propagation:	Division in spring or late fall
Problems:	Occasionally powdery mildew is found on the species.
Insider's tips:	This bold beauty is a very popular perennial for making a late summer statement. It is not easily divided, requiring a lot of back strength.
Combines with:	*Helenium autumnale, Rudbeckia fulgida* x *sullivantii* "Goldsturm", *Miscanthus sinensis* 'Malepartus', *Boltonia asteroides* 'Snowbank', *Buddleia davidii* 'Royal Red'

Euphorbia corollata
PRAIRIE SPURGE, PRAIRIE BABY'S BREATH

Plant type:	Perennial, native, drought-tolerant **Zone:** 4–8
Flower:	White stars branching out into clouds of bloom
Foliage:	Jade green, typical spurgelike leaves turn red in fall
Bloom length:	8 weeks
Height:	18–24 inches **Width/spacing:** 12 inches
Light:	Full sun **Soil:** Average to rich, evenly moist
Care:	Easy
Uses:	Prairie/meadow, weaver in the border, easy care, cut flower
Propagation:	Tip cuttings in early summer
Problems:	Needs other plants to "lean" on
Insider's tips:	A little-noticed prairie wildflower until it blooms! I would like to see this used more in the traditional border as an easy-care "baby's breath."
Combines with:	*Rudbeckia fulgida* var. *sullivantii* 'Goldsturm', *Sporobolus heterolepsis*, *Veronica* 'Sunny Border Blue', *Asclepias tuberosa*

Gaillardia x *grandiflora* 'Goblin'
GOBLIN BLANKET FLOWER

Plant type:	Perennial **Zone:** 3–9
Flower:	Deep red daisy with golden yellow-tipped petals
Foliage:	Dwarf, leafy mound; not sprawling like native species
Bloom length:	12 weeks
Height:	12 inches **Width/spacing:** 18 inches
Light:	Full sun **Soil:** Rich, moist, well-drained
Care:	Deadhead for continued bloom; no staking necessary
Uses:	Front of the border, bright accent, long bloomer, cottage garden, cut flower, prairie/meadow
Propagation:	Division in spring for rejuvenation after three years; seed
Problems:	Short-lived
Insider's tips:	The bright color scares many gardeners. Create excitement on the edge of your border with cautious use of companion plants—and you probably don't want to use this next to pink.
Combines with:	*Coreopsis verticillata* 'Zagreb', *Lychnis chalcedonica*, *Sporobolus heterolepsis*, *Veronica spicata* 'Blue Charm', *Euphorbia corollata*

Heliopsis helianthoides 'Summer Sun'
SUMMER SUN FALSE SUNFLOWER

Plant type:	Perennial, shrublike **Zone:** 3–9
Flower:	Golden yellow, 2-inch semi-double daisy
Foliage:	Masses of stems with pointed leaves along stems; gives a shrubby appearance
Bloom length:	10–13 weeks
Height:	4–5 feet **Width/spacing:** 3 feet
Light:	Sun to light shade **Soil:** Average, well-drained; will tolerate dry
Care:	Deadhead for extended bloom
Uses:	Back of the border, prairie/meadow, cut flower, attracts butterflies
Propagation:	Division in spring
Problems:	Occasionally needs support
Insider's tips:	This trouble-free long bloomer is a mainstay of the late summer garden.
Combines with:	*Liatris spicata* 'Kobold', *Veronica spicata* 'Blue Charm', *Lilium* x 'Casablanca', *Miscanthus sinensis* 'Strictus', *Clematis terniflora*, *Platycodon grandiflorus* 'Mariesii'

Hibiscus moscheutos 'Lord Baltimore'
LORD BALTIMORE ROSE MALLOW

Plant type:	Perennial, shrublike **Zone:** 5–9
Flower:	Red, 6- to 8-inch, saucer-shaped blossoms
Foliage:	Vase-shaped; shrubby with big, triangular leaves
Bloom length:	8–10 weeks
Height:	3–5 feet **Width/spacing:** 4 feet
Light:	Sun to light shade **Soil:** Rich, moist, well-drained
Care:	Deadhead for neatness, as flowers last only one day
Uses:	Architectural accent, background, screening, bold contrast
Propagation:	Softwood cuttings from May to July
Problems:	White flies, Japanese beetles
Insider's tips:	This plant is a stunner in the perennial border—a large "exclamation point"! The almost woody stems can be cut down for winter or before new growth in the spring.
Combines with:	*Patrinia scabiosifolia, Artemisia lactiflora, Miscanthus sinensis* 'Purpurescens', *Sorghastrum nutans* 'Sioux Blue', *Helenium autumnale, Eupatorium maculatum* 'Gateway'

Kalimeris pinnatifida (*Asteromoea mongolica*)
DOUBLE JAPANESE ASTER

Plant type:	Perennial **Zone:** 5–8
Flower:	Small, semi-double white daisy (aster)
Foliage:	Fine-textured, lancelike, light green leaves with heavily branched stems
Bloom length:	10-plus weeks
Height:	24 inches **Width/spacing:** 20 inches, spreading
Light:	Sun to part shade **Soil:** Rich, moist, well-drained
Care:	Easy; repeats bloom without deadheading
Uses:	Weaver and blender, mid-border, long bloomer, cottage garden, cut flower, attracts butterflies
Propagation:	Division in spring or fall
Problems:	Flops with too much shade; colonizes readily
Insider's tips:	*Kalimeris* is an adaptable and reliably long-blooming garden filler, even without deadheading.
Combines with:	*Lilium* x 'Stargazer', *Veronica* 'Sunny Border Blue', *Lychnis chalcedonica*, *Gaillardia* x *grandiflora* 'Goblin', *Heliopsis helianthoides* 'Summer Sun'

Lobelia cardinalis
CARDINAL FLOWER

Plant type: Perennial, native   **Zone:** 2–9

Flower: Intense red, tube-shaped and lipped, form a spike

Foliage: Upright; pointed leaves get smaller as they go up stems

Bloom length: 7–8 weeks

Height: 3–4 feet   **Width/spacing:** 18–24 inches

Light: Light shade, morning sun   **Soil:** Rich, moist

Care: Do not smother with mulch over winter, as plants are likely to die; deadhead for neatness

Uses: Wet garden, damp meadow, prairie, attracts butterflies and hummingbirds, woodland edge

Propagation: Divide in spring; self-sows

Problems: Short-lived; allow some seeding

Insider's tips: I have trouble getting this one to come back, and I have also found that the burgundy-foliaged ones are not hardy in my Zone 5 garden! Watch out for hummingbirds—even while shopping at the nursery!

Combines with: *Hosta montana* 'Aureo-marginata', *Lobelia siphilitica*, *Onoclea sensibilis*, *Hosta* 'Piedmont Gold', *Astilbe* x *arendsii* 'White Gloria'

Malva alcea 'Fastigiata'
HOLLYHOCK MALLOW

Plant type:	Perennial, drought-tolerant **Zone:** 4–7
Flower:	Light pink to rose-pink, like a 1-inch hollyhock bloom; heavy bloomer
Foliage:	Nicely lobed, many stemmed from basal crown
Bloom length:	10 weeks
Height:	2–3 feet **Width/spacing:** 30–36 inches
Light:	Sun to light shade **Soil:** Average, well-drained
Care:	Deadheading prolongs bloom as well a prevents seeding about
Uses:	Cottage garden, naturalizes, heavy bloomer, shrubby border plant
Propagation:	Self-sows
Problems:	Often needs staking; may die out in some areas but reseeds profusely if not deadheaded
Insider's tips:	I remember this as an old-fashioned plant from my grandmother's garden. If you don't want too much of a good thing, deadheading is mandatory!
Combines with:	*Leucanthemum vulgare, Hemerocallis* 'Hyperion', *Perovskia atriplicifolia, Salvia* x *superba* 'May Night', *Leucanthemum* x *superbum* 'Aglaia', *Kalimeris pinnatifida*

Patrinia scabiosifolia
PATRINIA

Plant type: Perennial   **Zone:** 5–8

Flower: Many small yellow flowers clustered similar to Queen Anne's lace

Foliage: Upright narrow habit; leaves reminiscent of a tall *Scabiosa*

Bloom length: 8 weeks

Height: 3–6 feet   **Width/spacing:** 24–30 inches

Light: Sun to light shade   **Soil:** Average, well-drained

Care: Deadhead for repeat bloom; does not need staking

Uses: Mid-border, blender, prairie/meadow, see-through plant

Propagation: Seed; long taproot not easily divided

Problems: Hard to find

Insider's tips: Purchased plants seem to vary widely in height (3 to 6 feet) . Try purchasing plants from only one source and refer to their height descriptions.

Combines with: *Helenium* (russet or red cultivars), *Hibiscus moscheutos* 'Lord Baltimore', *Veronica spicata* 'Blue Charm', *Caryopteris* x *clandonensis* 'Longwood Blue', *Echinacea purpurea* 'White Swan'

Perovskia atriplicifolia
RUSSIAN SAGE

Plant type:	Perennial, shrublike **Zone:** 4–9
Flower:	Soft, blue spikes, airy
Foliage:	Silver-gray, fragrant, branching
Bloom length:	12 weeks **Height:** 3–5 feet **Width/spacing:** 30–36 inches
Light:	Full sun
Soil:	Average to poor, well-drained; must have good drainage
Care:	Do not fertilize; if cutting back for winter, cut back to 12 inches; cut back stems by half in early summer for stouter plants (this also delays the bloom time)
Uses:	Cut flower, herb garden, mid-border, late summer color, foliage color
Propagation:	Offshoots often occur after three years
Problems:	Tends to become floppy
Insider's tips:	I have grown other cultivars reputed to be more upright without much luck. New 'Little Spire' is my next to try. Russian sage combines well with all plants, softening even the harshest orange and gold!
Combines with:	*Pennisetum alopecuroides, Rosa* 'Carefree Delight', *Rudbeckia fulgida* var. *sullivantii* 'Goldsturm', *Echinacea purpurea* 'Magnus', *Hemerocallis* 'Rocket City'

Phlox paniculata 'Bright Eyes'
BRIGHT EYES GARDEN PHLOX

Plant type:	Perennial **Zone:** 3–9
Flower:	Clusters of fragrant, clear pink florets with a deep rose center
Foliage:	Upright, sturdy stems with dark green, lancelike leaves
Bloom length:	7–10 weeks
Height:	24–30 inches **Width/spacing:** 24 inches
Light:	Sun to light shade **Soil:** Rich, moist, well-drained
Care:	Deadhead for repeat September bloom
Uses:	Mid-border, cottage garden, long bloomer, fragrance, cut flower
Propagation:	Offshoots can be divided in spring.
Problems:	Powdery mildew
Insider's tips:	Although moderately mildew resistant, Bright Eyes is more likely to suffer mildew during a drier summer. Start using a fungicidal soap in early June and repeat every two weeks. Remember to also dredge the soil surrounding infected plants to keep from splashing the fungal spores back onto the foliage.
Combines with:	*Perovskia atriplicifolia, Helictotrichon sempervirens, Rosa* 'Knock Out', *Artemisia ludoviciana* 'Valerie Finnis', *Platycodon grandiflorus* 'Mariesii'

Phlox paniculata 'David'
DAVID GARDEN PHLOX

Plant type:	Perennial **Zone:** 3–9
Flower:	Clusters of fragrant, long-blooming white florets
Foliage:	Upright and sturdy
Bloom length:	7–10 weeks
Height:	36–40 inches **Width/spacing:** 24 inches
Light:	Sun to light shade **Soil:** Rich, moist, well-drained
Care:	Supply extra fertilizer or compost
Uses:	Background, cottage garden, important border plant, fragrance, long bloomer
Propagation:	Division of offshoots after three years
Problems:	Although one of the most mildew-resistant varieties, it occasionally may need to be treated with fungicidal soap.
Insider's tips:	In my lightly shaded garden, 'David' can still be blooming in October! I have never needed to stake this plant.
Combines with:	*Perovskia atriplicifolia, Caryopteris* x *clandonensis* 'Longwood Blue', *Rudbeckia fulgida* var. *sullivantii* 'Goldsturm', *Liatris spicata* 'Kobold', *Echinacea purpurea*

Phlox paniculata 'Eva Cullum'
EVA CULLUM GARDEN PHLOX

Plant type:	Perennial **Zone:** 4–8
Flower:	Clusters of fragrant, hot pink florets with a darker eye form a larger bloom head (truss)
Foliage:	Upright leafy stems
Bloom length:	8–10 weeks
Height:	24–30 inches **Width/spacing:** 24 inches
Light:	Sun to light shade **Soil:** Rich, moist, well-drained
Care:	Deadhead for repeat bloom in September
Uses:	Cottage garden, cut flower, showy color in the border, mid-border, fragrance, long bloomer
Propagation:	Offshoots can be divided in spring
Problems:	None
Insider's tips:	I love the mildew resistance! Care should be taken in mixing other pinks close to this phlox.
Combines with:	*Macleaya cordata, Eupatorium maculatum* 'Gateway', *Perovskia atriplicifolia, Echinacea purpurea* 'White Swan', *Leucanthemum* x *superbum* 'Snowcap', *Kalimeris pinnatifida*

Phlox paniculata 'Fairest One'
FAIREST ONE GARDEN PHLOX

Plant type: Perennial **Zone:** 4–8

Flower: Light salmon-pink florets with a darker eye clustered to form a domed flower

Foliage: Upright and sturdy

Bloom length: 7–10 weeks

Height: 24 inches **Width/spacing:** 24 inches

Light: Sun to light shade **Soil:** Rich, moist, well-drained

Care: Deadhead for neatness and repeat bloom

Uses: Cottage garden, cut flower, showy color in the border, mid-border, fragrance

Propagation: Division of offshoots after three years

Problems: Occasional powdery mildew

Insider's tips: This is a noticeably shorter phlox and provides a different color of pink to the border.

Combines with: *Sedum* x 'Autumn Joy', *Platycodon grandiflorus* 'Sentimental Blue', *Euphorbia corollata, Campanula carpatica* 'Deep Blue Clips', *Filipendula ulmaria* 'Aurea'

Rudbeckia fulgida var. *sullivantii* 'Goldsturm'
BLACK-EYED SUSAN

Plant type:	Perennial **Zone:** 4–9
Flower:	Golden-yellow daisy with bronze-black central cone
Foliage:	Clump-forming, rough-textured
Bloom length:	10 weeks
Height:	24–36 inches **Width/spacing:** 24 inches
Light:	Full sun, tolerates shade **Soil:** Average, well-drained
Care:	If left for winter interest, dig out any seedlings in the spring
Uses:	Border, massed, attracts butterflies, brightens shady areas, winter interest
Propagation:	Division; self-sows
Problems:	Can be an aggressive reseeder
Insider's tips:	This is an overused perennial that can take over a garden. I like it best in shadier sites, where it seems softer and brings in much needed color for the late summer shade garden.
Combines with:	*Perovskia atriplicifolia, Sedum* x 'Autumn Joy', *Veronica* 'Sunny Border Blue', *Echinacea purpurea* 'White Swan', *Miscanthus sinensis* 'Strictus'

Rudbeckia nitida 'Herbstsonne'
HERBSTSONNE BLACK-EYED SUSAN

Plant type:	Perennial **Zone:** 3–8
Flower:	Soft, golden-yellow daisy with greenish central cone
Foliage:	Rich, glossy green basal mound with tall upright stems
Bloom length:	10 weeks
Height:	6–7 feet **Width/spacing:** 36 inches
Light:	Full sun **Soil:** Average, well-drained
Care:	Easy
Uses:	Back of the border, mixed border, architectural impact, insect and disease-resistant, attracts butterflies
Propagation:	Division in spring
Problems:	Occasionally needs staking
Insider's tips:	I like the softer flower color and different habit of this rudbeckia. Its large stature requires a large garden and taller planting partners.
Combines with:	*Phlox paniculata* 'David', *Perovskia atriplicifolia*, *Miscanthus sinensis* 'Strictus', *Hemerocallis* 'Rocket City', *Hibiscus moscheutos* 'Lord Baltimore'

Thalictrum rochebrunianum
LAVENDER MIST MEADOWRUE

Plant type: Perennial   **Zone:** 4–7

Flower: Tiny rosy-lavender flowers form an airy cloud

Foliage: Green, fine texture typical of the meadow rues; reddish stems

Bloom length: 6 weeks

Height: 4–5 feet   **Width/spacing:** 30–36 inches

Light: Light shade to part shade   **Soil:** Rich, moist

Care: Stake to support flower head

Uses: Woodland edge, background, architectural accent, border, cottage garden

Propagation: Division in spring; plants are often slow to recover.

Problems: May need staking

Insider's tips: This needs a good background, such as evergreens, to highlight the flowers. Bold foliage used as a companion sets off the fine texture of this meadow rue.

Combines with: *Cimicifuga racemosa, Phlox paniculata* 'David', *Kirengeshoma palmata, Chelone lyonii, Hosta fluctuans* 'Sagae'

CHAPTER 6

August

*Hot Colors Add to
the Sizzle of Summer*

Actaea rubra
RED BANEBERRY

Plant type:	Perennial, native **Zone:** 3–8
Flower:	Fuzzy white flowers clustered in rounded spikes become red berries in August
Foliage:	Deep green, similar to a loosely mounded astilbe
Bloom length:	2–3 weeks
Height:	30 to 36 inches **Width/spacing:** 24 inches
Light:	Part shade, shade **Soil:** Rich, moist, acidic
Care:	Easy
Uses:	Woodland, architectural accent, naturalistic garden, attractive berries
Propagation:	Division in spring; seedlings slow to develop
Problems:	Berries and roots are poisonous.
Insider's tips:	By now you have noticed that these are berries and not flowers. This is the *most* ornamental stage of red baneberry, which makes it look like Christmas in August!
Combines with:	Berries with: *Onoclea sensibilis, Aconitum carmichaelii, Lobelia cardinalis,* hostas. Flowers with: *Aquilegia* species, *Uvularia grandiflora, Trillium grandiflorum*

Allium senescens 'Glaucum'
ALLIUM, ORNAMENTAL ONION

Plant type:	Perennial, bulb **Zone:** 3–9
Flower:	Mauve to rose flowers cluster to form a ball
Foliage:	Blue-gray whorls of straplike leaves
Bloom length:	4 weeks
Height:	8–10 inches **Width/spacing:** 12 inches
Light:	Full sun **Soil:** Average, well-drained
Care:	Deadhead to prevent self-seeding
Uses:	Edger, rock garden, unusual foliage color and form
Propagation:	Division when clumps go dormant
Problems:	None
Insider's tips:	I like alliums that bloom in late summer and fall because ripening foliage is not a problem. Foliage declines with other non-evergreen perennials.
Combines with:	*Caryopteris* x *clandonensis* 'Longwood Blue', *Nepeta mussinii* 'Blue Wonder', *Heuchera* 'Plum Pudding', *Geranium sanguineum* var. *striatum, Sedum* x 'Ruby Glow'

Allium tuberosum
GARLIC CHIVES

Plant type:	Bulb, herb **Zone:** 3–8
Flower:	Ball of starry white flowers; rose-scented—amazing for the onion family!
Foliage:	Grasslike
Bloom length:	3–4 weeks
Height:	18 inches **Width/spacing:** 12 inches
Light:	Full sun **Soil:** Average, well-drained
Care:	Deadhead as flowers fade to prevent seeding about
Uses:	Herb or vegetable garden, edger, border, late season white flower
Propagation:	Division anytime; transplant self-sown seedlings, which take two years to bloom
Problems:	Seeds about prolifically
Insider's tips:	The white flowers perk-up the late summer garden. Regularly deadhead this chive or you will have it all over the garden. The foliage is used in cooking and has a pungent garlic smell when crushed.
Combines with:	*Rosa* cultivars, *Aster novae-angliae* 'Purple Dome', *Solidago* x 'Golden Baby', *Rudbeckia fulgida* var. *sullivantii* 'Goldsturm', *Caryopteris* x *clandonensis* 'Longwood Blue'

Anaphalis triplinervis 'Summer Snow'
SUMMER SNOW PEARLY EVERLASTING, THREE-VEINED EVERLASTING

Plant type: Perennial, evergreen, groundcover   **Zone:** 3–9

Flower: Small, white, furry buttons

Foliage: Silvery stems with woolly, silver-gray leaves

Bloom length: 3–4 weeks

Height: 12–18 inches   **Width/spacing:** 24 inches

Light: Sun to part shade

Soil: Moist (unlike most silver-leaved plants), well-drained

Care: Do not over fertilize

Uses: Groundcover, edger, foliage color, cottage garden, herb garden, dried flower

Propagation: Division in spring every three to four years to rejuvenate and remove old woody crowns

Problems: Will loose lower leaves in dry soils

Insider's tips: Finally, a silver plant that does well in moist soils—even in a bit of shade! Taller pearly everlastings tend to flop. Note that this cultivar is also a better white than the species.

Combines with: *Rosa* 'Flower Carpet', *Veronica alpina* 'Goodness Grows', *Aster novae-angliae* 'Purple Dome'

Artemisia lactiflora
WHITE MUGWORT, GHOST PLANT

Plant type: Perennial   **Zone:** 3–8

Flower: Creamy white plumes 1 to 2 feet long

Foliage: Tall stems bear green, toothed leaves from a basal rosette

Bloom length: 6–8 weeks

Height: 4–6 feet   **Width/spacing:** 3–4 feet

Light: Sun to light shade   **Soil:** Average to rich, evenly moist

Care: Needs soil moisture, unlike most artemisias

Uses: Dried flower, back of the border, cottage garden, herb garden, mixed border

Propagation: Stem cuttings in early summer

Problems: May require staking

Insider's tips: Unlike other artemisias, the foliage is not silver and the plant needs moist soil. The profuse creamy plumes make a great background for the hot colors of late summer!

Combines with: *Helenium autumnale* 'Butterpat', *Alcea rosea, Hibiscus moscheutos* 'Lord Baltimore', *Macleaya cordata, Rudbeckia nitida* 'Herbstsonne', *Miscanthus sinensis* 'Strictus'

Astilbe chinensis 'Pumila'
PUMILA ASTILBE, CHINESE ASTILBE

Plant type:	Perennial, groundcover **Zone:** 4–9
Flower:	Lavender-rose with very upright spikes
Foliage:	Bronze-green mats of typical astilbe foliage
Bloom length:	4 weeks
Height:	8–10 inches **Width/spacing:** 12 inches
Light:	Part shade, shade **Soil:** Rich, moist
Care:	Do not allow to dry out
Uses:	Groundcover, late-blooming astilbe, edger, shade garden, water's edge, wet garden
Propagation:	Division in spring
Problems:	None
Insider's tips:	Some newer introductions—'Veronica Klose' and 'Visions'—are taller and have showier flower color.
Combines with:	*Hosta* 'Halcyon', *Hosta* 'Golden Tiara', *Chelone lyonii, Athyrium filix-femina*

Carex elata (*stricta*) 'Bowles Golden'
BOWLES GOLDEN GRASS, TUFTED SEDGE

Plant type:	Ornamental grass **Zone:** 5–8
Flower:	Brownish tufts that are barely noticeable
Foliage:	Yellow with narrow green edge, upright thin blades gently arch at the tips
Bloom length:	4-plus weeks
Height:	24 inches **Width/spacing:** 18 inches
Light:	Part shade, shade **Soil:** Average to rich, evenly moist
Care:	You may cut it back if it doesn't withstand winter conditions.
Uses:	Accent, winter interest, brightens shade, woodland edge
Propagation:	Division in spring
Problems:	None
Insider's tips:	I have had best luck with this plant in sites having only spring sunlight.
Combines with:	*Hosta sieboldiana* 'Frances Williams', *Asarum europaeum*, *Polystichum acrostichoides*, *Galium odoratum*, *Epimedium* x *versicolor* 'Sulphureum'

Caryopteris x *clandonensis* 'Longwood Blue'
LONGWOOD BLUE SHRUB, BLUEBEARD

Plant type:	Perennial, shrublike, drought-tolerant **Zone:** 5–9
Flower:	Spirea-like lavender-blue clusters in leaf axles
Foliage:	Gray-green, shrubby, fragrant
Bloom length:	7 weeks, sometimes more
Height:	2–3 feet **Width/spacing:** 3 feet
Light:	Sun to light shade **Soil:** Average, well-drained
Care:	Prune back to live wood in spring; use a winter mulch in Zone 5
Uses:	Mixed border, cottage garden, herb garden, late-season bloom
Propagation:	Root stem cuttings in spring
Problems:	Acts like a dieback shrub in the North; not reliably hardy in Zone 5
Insider's tips:	The lavender-blue flowers look spectacular next to shrubs like crimson barberry. Consider some of the darker blue selections: 'Arthur Simmonds', 'Dark Knight', and 'Kew Blue'.
Combines with:	*Rudbeckia fulgida* var. *sullivantii* 'Goldsturm', *Silphium perfoliatum*, *Rosa* 'Showbiz', *Miscanthus sinensis* 'Morning Light', *Lilium* x 'Casablanca', *Echinacea purpurea* 'Magnus'

Chelone lyonii
TURTLE HEAD

Plant type:	Perennial, native **Zone:** 3–8
Flower:	Carmine-rose, hooded, resembles turtle's head; in clusters that form a spike
Foliage:	Noticeably dark green leaves along upright stems
Bloom length:	4-plus weeks
Height:	2–3 feet **Width/spacing:** 2 feet
Light:	Part shade, shade; tolerates sun in moist areas
Soil:	Rich, moist **Care:** Easy
Uses:	Woodland edge, mid-border, late-season bloom, wet/stream garden, wet meadow, attracts butterflies, cut flower
Propagation:	Division in spring
Problems:	None
Insider's tips:	Turtle head's dark leaves are showy even in the shade—as are the flowers. I have tried the new cultivar 'Hot Lips' but cannot tell the difference! They are supposed to have red stems, but mine don't. Turtle head resembles snapdragon and should delight any child.
Combines with:	*Hosta* 'Antioch', *Hosta* 'Golden Scepter', *Onoclea sensibilis, Carex elata* 'Bowles Golden', *Anemone* x *hybrida* 'Honorine Jobert', *Lobelia siphilitica, Eupatorium coelestinum*

Cimicifuga ramosa 'Atropurpurea'
PURPLE-FOLIAGED SNAKEROOT

Plant type:	Perennial **Zone:** 3–9
Flower:	Fragrant, purple-tinged white fluffy spikes
Foliage:	Broad clumps with divided purple-tinged leaves and stems; much like an elegant astilbe
Bloom length:	4–6 weeks
Height:	4–6 feet **Width/spacing:** 3 feet
Light:	Shade; will tolerate a little sun **Soil:** Rich, moist
Care:	Easy; leave seed heads for late-season interest
Uses:	Foliage color, back of the border, shade garden, wildflower garden, architectural accent, attractive seed heads, attracts butterflies, wet garden
Propagation:	Division, but this has a long taproot and does not divide easily
Problems:	Must have consistent soil moisture—will be stunted in drier soils; if seed-grown, select plants for best-colored foliage
Insider's tips:	At the nursery, choose the darkest purple leaves you can find! The Blooms of Bressingham selection 'Brunette' is a 3- to 4-foot plant with consistently bronzed leaves.
Combines with:	*Polygonatum odoratum* 'Variegatum', *Hosta* 'Piedmont Gold', *Hosta* 'Antioch', *Kirengeshoma palmata*

Cimicifuga ramosa 'Hillside Black Beauty'
HILLSIDE BLACK BEAUTY SNAKEROOT

Plant type:	Perennial **Zone:** 4–8
Flower:	Fragrant, white, more of a spike than 'Atropurpurea'
Foliage:	Reliably dark purple leaves
Bloom length:	4–6 weeks
Height:	5–6 feet **Width/spacing:** 3 feet
Light:	Part shade, shade **Soil:** Rich, moist
Care:	Easy, as long as it has plenty of soil moisture
Uses:	Foliage color, back of the border, shade garden, wildflower garden, architectural accent, attractive seed heads, attracts butterflies, wet garden, fragrance
Propagation:	A patented perennial—do not propagate
Problems:	None
Insider's tips:	'Hillside Black Beauty' is the darkest American selection with reliable foliage color. It comes from Fred and Mary Ann McGourty of Hillside Gardens, Connecticut.
Combines with:	*Hosta* 'Piedmont Gold', *Hosta* 'Albo-Marginata', *Macleaya cordata, Lobelia siphilitica, Lobelia cardinalis*

Clematis terniflora (paniculata) 'Sweet Autumn'
SWEET AUTUMN CLEMATIS

Plant type:	Perennial, vine **Zone:** 4–8
Flower:	Thousands of fragrant, white, four-petaled stars; can look like a huge cascading bridal bouquet
Foliage:	Vine, quickly covers a fence or small tree
Bloom length:	4 weeks **Height:** 10–20 feet **Width/spacing:** 12–18 inches
Light:	Sun to light shade **Soil:** Rich, moist, well-drained
Care:	Prune in half to shape in spring after buds swell (usually late March in the North)
Uses:	Fence or wall, trellis, background for border
Propagation:	I have never tried—I'm too busy training what I have!
Problems:	Needs root zone to be shaded so soil stays cool and moist
Insider's tips:	This clematis has the quickest growth—about ten feet in a year! You practically need knitting needles to train this fast-grower; cup hooks on wooden structures can help. Daylilies are a good companion to shade the root zone.
Combines with:	*Heliopsis helianthoides* 'Summer Sun', *Thalictrum flavum* 'Glaucum', *Rudbeckia nitida* 'Herbstsonne', *Delphinium* x *elatum, Alcea rosea*

Eupatorium coelestinum
HARDY AGERATUM, MIST FLOWER

Plant type: Perennial, native, herb   **Zone:** 5–10

Flower: Blue, fluffy, ageratum-like

Foliage: Tall ageratum

Bloom length: 4–6 weeks   **Height:** 24 inches   **Width/spacing:** 18 inches

Light: Sun to part shade (especially in hottest part of the day)

Soil: Average, well-drained

Care: Rogue out seedlings in spring

Uses: Blue garden, softens autumn colors, mid-border, wildflower, wood-land edge, attracts butterflies

Propagation: Division in spring; self-sows vigorously

Problems: Sometimes floppy or weedy

Insider's tips: If cut back in half in early June, plants will be shorter, bushier, and less likely to flop over. The cultivar 'Wayside Variety' is reported to be shorter with more flowers.

Combines with: *Rudbeckia fulgida* var. *sullivantii* 'Goldsturm', *Anemone* x *hybrida* 'Honorine Jobert', *Lobelia cardinalis, Sedum* x 'Autumn Joy', *Aster lateriflorus* 'Horizontalis'

Hakonechloa macra 'Aureola'

JAPANESE COMBED GRASS

Plant type:	Ornamental grass **Zone:** 6–8
Flower:	Soft and airy inflorescence
Foliage:	Yellow-and-green variegated mounds arch to one side as if combed
Bloom length:	3 weeks
Height:	12 inches **Width/spacing:** 24 inches
Light:	Part shade; morning sun
Soil:	Rich, moist, well-drained, slightly acidic
Care:	Cut back in late winter; it benefits from a winter compost mulch in the North
Uses:	Brightens woodland or shady garden, adds unusual texture, rock garden accent, pot garden
Propagation:	Division; this is a very slow grower, so I recommend buying new plants.
Problems:	Not rated hardy for Zone 5
Insider's tips:	It occasionally does not overwinter in my Zone 5 garden. Other gardeners in my area have had good luck, and I have seen it grown further north at Boerner Botanic Garden in southern Wisconsin.
Combines with:	*Polygonatum commutatum, Hosta* 'Gold Standard', *Dryopteris marginalis, Epimedium* x *versicolor* 'Sulphureum', *Hosta* 'Halcyon'

Helenium autumnale 'Butterpat'
BUTTERPAT HELEN'S FLOWER, SNEEZEWEED

Plant type:	Perennial **Zone:** 3–7
Flower:	Butter-yellow daisy with a buttonlike center; prolific
Foliage:	Rugged, heavily branched
Bloom length:	6 weeks
Height:	30–36 inches **Width/spacing:** 18 inches
Light:	Full sun **Soil:** Average to rich, evenly moist
Care:	Easy; does not need pinching for branching
Uses:	Background, fall color, cottage garden, accent
Propagation:	Division in spring every three years
Problems:	Taller varieties may need staking; powdery mildew may be a problem for the species.
Insider's tips:	Many new cultivars are available in red, rust, yellow, and gold. Look for shorter, sturdier plants that do not require staking.
Combines with:	*Eupatorium coelestinum, Miscanthus sinensis* 'Purpurescens', *Miscanthus sinensis* 'Strictus', *Artemisia lactiflora*

Hosta 'Halcyon'
HALCYON BLUE HOSTA

Plant type:	Perennial **Zone:** 3–9
Flower:	Rich lavender nodding bells heavily clumped along stems
Foliage:	Rounded, blue leaves in dense mounds
Bloom length:	4–6 weeks
Height:	16 inches **Width/spacing:** 24 inches
Light:	Part shade, shade **Soil:** Average, well-drained to moist
Care:	Easy; slug-resistant foliage
Uses:	Groundcover, specimen, massed, mixed border, edger, shade garden, rock garden, cut flower, late-blooming hosta
Propagation:	Division in spring when plants have increased in size
Problems:	Deer-browse
Insider's tips:	Flowers and blue foliage make a stunning combination! Notice that the flowers look like a bouquet. If you aren't fond of hosta flowers, cut them for indoor arrangements—hosta flowers last for two weeks in water.
Combines with:	*Hakonechloa macra* 'Aureola', *Kirengeshoma palmata, Onoclea sensibilis, Lamium maculatum* 'White Nancy', *Astilbe japonica* 'Rheinland'

Kirengeshoma palmata
YELLOW WAXBELLS

Plant type: Perennial **Zone:** 5–7

Flower: Yellow, waxy shuttlecocks

Foliage: Shrubby with bold, maplelike leaves

Bloom length: 4–6 weeks

Height: 36 inches **Width/spacing:** 24–30 inches

Light: Part shade **Soil:** Average to rich, evenly moist

Care: Easy, as long as soil moisture is maintained

Uses: Naturalistic, woodland, background, accent

Propagation: Plants are best left undisturbed

Problems: When pushed into too much shade, it will dwindle to a small-sized plant, sometimes without bloom

Insider's tips: A wonderful "substantial" plant for part shade! Waxbells are used in English gardens, and I often wonder why they are not grown more in the U.S.

Combines with: *Sedum* x 'Autumn Joy', *Dicentra* x 'Luxuriant', *Tricyrtis hirta*, *Lamium maculatum* 'Beedham's White', *Viola labradorica*

Lilium henryi 'Black Beauty'
BLACK BEAUTY AURELIAN HYBRID LILY

Plant type: Bulb   **Zone:** 4–7

Flower: Deep crimson, recurved petals are edge in white, with many flowers along tall stems

Foliage: Glossy, dark green leaves arranged in a very architectural pattern

Bloom length: 4–6 weeks

Height: 5–7 feet   **Width/spacing:** 18 inches

Light: Full sun   **Soil:** Average, well-drained

Care: Stake as buds appear, remove flowers as they fade

Uses: Late-season lily, architectural accent, cottage garden, back of the border, specimen

Propagation: Divide bulblets after blooming, planting at least 8 inches deep

Problems: Needs staking

Insider's tips: What an "exclamation mark" this lily makes! It is great for extending the bloom season of lilies.

Combines with: *Hibiscus moscheutos* 'Lord Baltimore', *Delphinium* x *elatum*, *Kalimeris pinnatifida*, *Patrinia scabiosifolia*, *Perovskia atriplicifolia*

Lobelia siphilitica
GREAT BLUE LOBELIA

Plant type:	Perennial, native **Zone:** 3–8
Flower:	Blue to violet tube-shaped and lipped clusters form a spike
Foliage:	Upright, clump-forming, leafy, slender stems
Bloom length:	5–6 weeks
Height:	24–30 inches **Width/spacing:** 18 inches
Light:	Part shade; prefers afternoon shade
Soil:	Rich, moist—tolerates drier soil
Care:	Be sure crown is buried deeply enough or whole plant topples
Uses:	Naturalistic, blue garden, prairie/meadow, woodland edge, shady border, cut flower, attracts butterflies
Propagation:	Division of basal offshoots in spring or fall; self-sows
Problems:	May need staking
Insider's tips:	I never met a lobelia that I didn't like! The new crosses are an array of jewel-tone colors with increasingly longer bloom times.
Combines with:	*Helenium autumnale, Hibiscus moscheutos* 'Lord Baltimore', *Hosta* 'Sum and Substance'; attractive with other colors of lobelias

Macleaya cordata
PLUME POPPY

Plant type:	Perennial **Zone:** 4–9
Flower:	Creamy white 12-inch plume
Foliage:	Architectural plant with large, lobed leaves with a somewhat bronze cast and chalky stems
Bloom length:	4 weeks
Height:	6–8 feet **Width/spacing:** 4-plus feet
Light:	Sun to part shade **Soil:** Average, well-drained
Care:	Contain; cut down in fall
Uses:	Screening, background, architectural accent, border, mixed border, cottage garden
Propagation:	Division in spring
Problems:	Very invasive
Insider's tips:	Some people claim this is less invasive in shadier sites. Consider using plume poppy only if you have the space to let it roam.
Combines with:	*Filipendula venusta* 'Rubra', *Miscanthus sinensis* 'Malepartus', *Rudbeckia nitida* 'Herbstsonne', *Hibiscus moscheutos* 'Lord Baltimore', *Helenium autumnale*

Physostegia virginiana 'Miss Manners'
MISS MANNERS OBEDIENT PLANT

Plant type:	Perennial **Zone:** 2–9
Flower:	White, very upright spike of snapdragon flowers
Foliage:	Spreading clump from which straight stems grow
Bloom length:	6–8 weeks
Height:	18 inches **Width/spacing:** 12–18 inches
Light:	Sun to part shade **Soil:** Average, well-drained
Care:	Deadhead for repeat bloom
Uses:	Cut flower, mid-border, massing, wildflower, meadow
Propagation:	Patented plant—do not propagate
Problems:	New introduction—it is hoped that it is not really invasive
Insider's tips:	In trials, this new obedient plant does not become a thug in the garden, and the white flowers are easy to use with the hot colors of late summer. Cultivar 'Summer Snow' is also less invasive.
Combines with:	*Phlox paniculata* 'Fairest One', *Rudbeckia fulgida* var. *sullivantii* 'Goldsturm', *Echinacea purpurea* 'Magnus', *Aster* x *frikartii* 'Monch'

Physostegia virginiana 'Vivid'

VIVID FALSE DRAGONHEAD, OBEDIENT PLANT

Plant type:	Perennial **Zone:** 2–9
Flower:	Bright pink spike looks like a pointed snapdragon
Foliage:	Spreading clump from which straight stems grow
Bloom length:	8 week
Height:	18–24 inches **Width/spacing:** 15 inches
Light:	Sun to part shade **Soil:** Average to poor, well-drained
Care:	Benefits from pinching back in early June; rogue out unwanted plants
Uses:	Cut flower, mid-border, massing, wildflower, meadow
Propagation:	Division in spring
Problems:	Invasive; rich soils produce floppy plants
Insider's tips:	Friend Stephanie Cohen calls this "disobedient plant"! *Physostegia* 'Variegata' has very nice white foliage variegation and is less vigorous.
Combines with:	*Anemone* x *hybrida* 'Alba', *Phlox paniculata* 'David', *Perovskia atriplicifolia*, *Caryopteris* x *clandonensis* 'Longwood Blue'

Sorghastrum nutans 'Sioux Blue'
SIOUX BLUE INDIAN GRASS

Plant type:	Ornamental grass **Zone:** 3–8
Flower:	Tan plumes at least 12 inches long
Foliage:	Gray-blue with upright habit
Bloom length:	6-plus weeks
Height:	4–6 feet **Width/spacing:** 30–36 inches
Light:	Sun to light shade **Soil:** Average to rich, evenly moist
Care:	Cut down in early spring before new growth
Uses:	Screening, massing, blue-colored foliage, winter interest, architectural accent
Propagation:	Division in spring
Problems:	None
Insider's tips:	This is a Longwood Gardens selection of a prairie native with better blue foliage.
Combines with:	*Eupatorium maculatum* 'Gateway', *Hibiscus moscheutos* 'Lord Baltimore', *Patrinia scabiosifolia, Helenium autumnale*

Veronicastrum virginicum
CULVER'S ROOT

Plant type:	Perennial, native, drought-tolerant **Zone:** 3–8
Flower:	White spikes in a whorl, like a heavy-blooming veronica
Foliage:	Upright and tall, leaves presented in a whorl
Bloom length:	4–6 weeks
Height:	5 feet **Width/spacing:** 3 feet
Light:	Sun to part shade **Soil:** Average to rich, evenly moist
Care:	Easy
Uses:	Back of the border, prairie, meadow, architectural accent, white garden, attracts butterflies
Propagation:	Division in spring
Problems:	Only needs staking if site is too shady
Insider's tips:	It helps to provide planting companions that the tall stems can "recline" on.
Combines with:	*Ligularia stenocephala* 'The Rocket', *Anemone* x *hybrida*, *Miscanthus sinensis* 'Nippon', *Eupatorium coelestinum*, *Eupatorium maculatum* 'Gateway'

Anemone vitifolia 'Robustissima'
GRAPELEAF ANEMONE

Plant type:	Perennial, groundcover **Zone:** 3–8
Flower:	Rosy-pink anemone flower with showy yellow stamens
Foliage:	Medium green, grapelike foliage in mounds to 18 inches
Bloom length:	6–8 weeks
Height:	36 inches **Width/spacing:** 36–40 inches
Light:	Sun to part shade **Soil:** Rich, moist, well-drained
Care:	Allow enough spacing
Uses:	Mixed border, late-season bloom, cut flower, cover bulbs, ground-cover
Propagation:	Division in spring
Problems:	Vigorous grower; may die out in the North in a dry winter without snow cover
Insider's tips:	This is the first fall anemone to bloom! Notice that I call it a groundcover—it spreads over time and should not be planted with perennials that can't take the competition.
Combines with:	*Aconitum carmichaelii, Lobelia siphilitica, Sedum* x 'Autumn Joy', *Veronicastrum virginicum, Tradescantia* x *andersoniana* 'Zwanenburg Blue'

Aster divaricatus
WHITE WOOD ASTER

Plant type:	Perennial, native **Zone:** 4–8
Flower:	¾-inch, starry, white daisy with a yellow center
Foliage:	Reclining, purple-black stems with heart-shaped leaves
Bloom length:	8 weeks
Height:	1–2 feet **Width/spacing:** 3 feet
Light:	Part shade, shade **Soil:** Rich, moist, well-drained
Care:	Cut back plants in early June for compactness and less sprawling
Uses:	Woodland edge, late-season bloom, cottage garden, profuse bloom
Propagation:	Division in spring
Problems:	Sprawls
Insider's tips:	I "discovered" this native aster while visiting English gardens! Add this aster to your shade garden to extend the bloom season in the shade.
Combines with:	*Hosta* 'Piedmont Gold', *Brunnera macrophylla, Eupatorium coelestinum, Rudbeckia fulgida* x *sullivantii* 'Goldsturm'

Boltonia asteroides 'Snowbank'
SNOWBANK BOLTONIA ASTER

Plant type: Perennial   **Zone:** 4–9

Flower: Masses of white, daisylike flowers with yellow centers

Foliage: Gray-green, upright/vase-shaped with tall stems

Bloom length: 8 weeks

Height: 4 feet   **Width/spacing:** 3 feet

Light: Sun to light shade   **Soil:** Average, well-drained

Care: Easy; does not need staking

Uses: Back of the border, structure, fall-bloom, attracts butterflies

Propagation: Division in spring of the many offshoots this plant can produce

Problems: None; I have not seen rabbit-browse on this asterlike plant

Insider's tips: *Boltonia asteroides* 'Pink Beauty' blooms earlier at three to four feet, but it needs staking.

Combines with: *Paeonia* cultivars, *Veronica spicata* 'Blue Charm', *Sedum* x 'Autumn Joy', *Calamogrostis* x *acutiflora* 'Karl Foerster', *Solidago rugosa* 'Fireworks', *Rudbeckia nitida* 'Herbstsonne'

Calamogrostis x *acutiflora* 'Karl Foerster'
FEATHER REED GRASS

Plant type:	Ornamental grass **Zone:** 5–9
Flower:	Wheat-colored to golden feathery inflorescence
Foliage:	Upright, vase-shaped clump of leaves
Bloom length:	8 weeks
Height:	4–6 feet **Width/spacing:** 3 feet
Light:	Sun to light shade **Soil:** Average to rich, evenly moist
Care:	Cut back in late winter (early April in the Midwest)
Uses:	Architectural accent, screening, winter interest, mixed border, new American garden
Propagation:	Division in spring
Problems:	None
Insider's tips:	Besides being one of the earliest ornamental grasses to bloom, it is easy to care for and requires low maintenance.
Combines with:	*Rudbeckia fulgida* x *sullivantii* 'Goldsturm', *Echinacea purpurea*, *Sedum* x 'Autumn Joy', *Alcea rosea*, *Perovskia atriplicifolia*

Ceratostigma plumbaginoides
LEADWORT

Plant type:	Perennial, groundcover **Zone:** 5–9
Flower:	Clusters of small, royal blue florets
Foliage:	Spreading foliage turns red-bronze in fall
Bloom length:	6 weeks
Height:	8 inches **Width/spacing:** 18 inches
Light:	Part shade, but I have seen it grown in full sun
Soil:	Average, well-drained
Care:	Mulch for winter in Zone 5
Uses:	Groundcover, edger, fall color, pot garden
Propagation:	Division in spring; stem cuttings
Problems:	Plant emerges in late spring
Insider's tips:	Leadwort is often overlooked until it blooms! Because it is so late to come up in the spring, take care not to dig it up.
Combines with:	*Heuchera* 'Plum Pudding', *Helictotrichon sempervirens, Artemisia stelleriana* 'Silver Brocade', *Solidago rugosa* 'Fireworks'

Eupatorium rugosum 'Chocolate'
CHOCOLATE WHITE SNAKEROOT

Plant type:	Perennial **Zone:** 3–7
Flower:	Fluffy, white flowers resemble white-flowered ageratum
Foliage:	Mounds of chocolate-tinged oval leaves
Bloom length:	6 weeks
Height:	36–40 inches **Width/spacing:** 3 feet
Light:	Sun to light shade; afternoon shade preferred
Soil:	Average, well-drained
Care:	Cut down for winter
Uses:	Foliage color, cottage garden, mid-border
Propagation:	Division in spring
Problems:	Watch for seeding about
Insider's tips:	This is a recent selection of the native snakeroot. It acts as a great dark background for summer-blooming plants, but it loses some of its foliage color at bloom time.
Combines with:	*Caryopteris* x *clandonensis* 'Longwood Blue', *Solidago rugosa* 'Fireworks', *Miscanthus sinensis* 'Nippon', *Aster* x *frikartii* 'Monch'

Geranium wallichianum 'Buxton's Variety'

BUXTON'S BLUE GERANIUM

Plant type: Perennial **Zone:** 3–8

Flower: Blue with a white center and upward-facing saucer

Foliage: White marbled foliage that trails on reddish stems

Bloom length: 8–10 weeks

Height: 6–8 inches **Width/spacing:** 12–15 inches

Light: Sun to part shade **Soil:** Rich, moist, well-drained

Care: Easy

Uses: Rock garden, long bloomer, late-season geranium, edger

Propagation: Root cuttings taken in late spring; seed

Problems: Difficult to find stock to buy!

Insider's tips: This is the *one* plant I have not been able to get for my garden because the mail-order nurseries always run out! I would love to have a geranium blooming from late summer into fall.

Combines with: *Sedum* x 'Autumn Joy', *Aster divaricatus*, *Aster lateriflorus* 'Horizontalis', *Allium tuberosum*, *Anaphalis triplinervis*

Miscanthus sinensis 'Kaskade'
CASCADE JAPANESE SILVER GRASS

Plant type:	Ornamental grass **Zone:** 5–9
Flower:	Golden tan tassels held well above the foliage
Foliage:	Wide, cascading dark green with a central white stripe
Bloom length:	10-plus weeks **Height:** 5–6 feet **Width/spacing:** 4 feet
Light:	Sun to light shade **Soil:** Average to rich, evenly moist
Care:	Cut to about 2 inches in late winter before new growth begins
Uses:	Screening, winter color/interest, bold architectural accent, new American garden
Propagation:	Division in spring (requires some strength to divide)
Problems:	None
Insider's tips:	Look closely at the different *Miscanthus* for height, shape, flower color, and winter interest, then decide which is best for your garden. An easy way to cut back the big ornamental grasses is to first tie up the foliage with twine and then cut it down to 2 inches from the ground. The entire bundle can be easily carried off for recycling. I have not had much luck composting the long grass foliage.
Combines with:	*Amsonia tabernaemontana, Anemone* x *hybrida* 'Honorine Jobert', *Rosa* 'Carefree Delight', *Aconitum carmichaelii, Eupatorium maculatum* 'Gateway'

Miscanthus sinensis 'Malepartus'
MALEPARTUS MAIDEN GRASS, EULALIA GRASS

Plant type:	Ornamental grass **Zone:** 5–9
Flower:	Large pink-purple plumes turn silver in the fall
Foliage:	Upright, dark green, slightly bronzed
Bloom length:	8-plus weeks
Height:	6–7 feet **Width/spacing:** 3 feet
Light:	Sun to light shade **Soil:** Average to rich, evenly moist
Care:	Cut to about 2 inches in late winter before new growth begins
Uses:	Screening, winter color/interest, bold architectural accent, new American garden
Propagation:	Division in spring
Problems:	None
Insider's tips:	Maiden grass selections have been bred recently for earlier bloom times and more colorful blooms. Read catalogs and plant labels carefully to select the succession of colors you want.
Combines with:	*Hibiscus moscheutos* 'Lord Baltimore', *Panicum virgatum* 'Rotstrahlbusch', *Lilium henryi* 'Black Beauty', *Macleaya cordata*

Miscanthus sinensis 'Nippon'
NIPPON JAPANESE SILVER GRASS

Plant type: Ornamental grass **Zone:** 5–9

Flower: Silvery-tan open plumes held 12 inches above foliage turn white in fall

Foliage: Slender, fine-textured green fountain

Bloom length: 6-plus weeks

Height: 3–4 feet **Width/spacing:** 3 feet

Light: Sun to light shade **Soil:** Average to rich, evenly moist

Care: Cut to about 2 inches in late winter before new growth begins

Uses: Mixed border, shorter ornamental grass, foliage color, architectural accent, winter interest

Propagation: Division in spring

Problems: None

Insider's tips: Another smaller-scaled maiden grass. Look closely at the different miscanthus for height, shape, flower color, and winter interest, then decide which is best for your garden.

Combines with: *Rosa rugosa, Solidago rugosa* 'Fireworks', *Heliopsis helianthoides* 'Summer Sun', *Aster* x *frikartii* 'Monch'

Miscanthus sinensis 'Purpurescens'
FLAME GRASS

Plant type:	Ornamental grass **Zone:** 5–9
Flower:	Reddish inflorescence aging to white cotton fluff
Foliage:	Very upright green grass turns red in late summer, then tannish-red for winter
Bloom length:	8-plus weeks
Height:	3–4 feet **Width/spacing:** 2 feet
Light:	Full sun **Soil:** Average to rich, evenly moist
Care:	Cut to about 2 inches in late winter before new growth begins
Uses:	Smaller-scaled grass, winter color/interest, bold architectural accent, massing, mixed border
Propagation:	Division in spring (requires some strength)
Problems:	None
Insider's tips:	This smaller-scaled maiden grass is excellent for the small garden. It has become one of my favorites, producing earlier outstanding fall color that continues well into winter.
Combines with:	*Sedum* x 'Autumn Joy', *Helenium autumnale*, *Rudbeckia nitida* 'Herbstsonne', *Caryopteris* x *clandonensis* 'Longwood Blue', *Rosa* 'Betty Prior' (shown in this picture with native sumac)

Panicum virgatum 'Rotstrahlbusch'
RED SWITCH GRASS

Plant type:	Ornamental grass, drought-tolerant **Zone:** 3–9
Flower:	Fine-textured reddish sprays, aging to wheat
Foliage:	Upright, clump-former whose leaves turn red in fall
Bloom length:	8-plus weeks
Height:	3 feet **Width/spacing:** 24–30 inches
Light:	Full sun **Soil:** Average, well-drained
Care:	Cut back in late winter
Uses:	Winter interest, background, mixed border, massing
Propagation:	Division early in the season
Problems:	None
Insider's tips:	All of the switch grasses give a fine-textured background for other perennials but vary as to color of blooms and foliage. Choose what is best for your garden.
Combines with:	*Heliopsis helianthoides* 'Summer Sun', *Echinacea purpurea* 'White Swan', *Liatris spicata* 'Kobold', *Solidago rugosa* 'Fireworks', *Boltonia asteroides* 'Snowbank'

Pennisetum alopecuroides
FOUNTAIN GRASS

Plant type:	Ornamental grass **Zone:** 4–9
Flower:	Pinkish, fuzzy bottlebrush, aging to wheat color
Foliage:	Green fountainlike mound turning wheat-colored in fall
Bloom length:	8-plus weeks
Height:	3–4 feet **Width/spacing:** 36–40 inches
Light:	Sun to part shade **Soil:** Average, well-drained
Care:	Cut down before new growth
Uses:	Mixed border, fountain form, winter interest, early blooming grass
Propagation:	Division late winter (requires strength)
Problems:	Inflorescence shatters in winter wind and rain; sometimes seeds into lawns
Insider's tips:	For the smaller garden, cultivar 'Hameln' is 2 feet and 'Little Bunny' is 1 foot. There is also a darker flower form—'Moudry'.
Combines with:	*Heuchera* 'Plum Pudding', *Echinacea purpurea* 'Magnus', *Rudbeckia fulgida* var. *sullivantii* 'Goldsturm', *Aster novae-angliae* 'Purple Dome'

Sedum x 'Autumn Joy'
AUTUMN JOY STONECROP

Plant type:	Perennial **Zone:** 3–9
Flower:	Rose color turns russet; broccoli-like buds are light green
Foliage:	Thick and fleshy, gray-blue
Bloom length:	12 weeks
Height:	18–24 inches **Width/spacing:** 30 inches
Light:	Full sun, but tolerates a good deal of shade
Soil:	Average to poor, well-drained
Care:	Benefits from pinching back in early June
Uses:	Border, massing, rock garden, textural highlight, winter interest, attracts butterflies
Propagation:	Stem cuttings; division
Problems:	Can rot with too much moisture
Insider's tips:	Many other sedums are worth looking at for interesting foliage or flower, but 'Autumn Joy' is the best for winter interest. I still like all growing stages of this plant—even the budding broccoli stage!
Combines with:	*Caryopteris* x *clandonensis* 'Longwood Blue', *Pennisetum alopecuroides, Echinacea purpurea, Boltonia asteroides* 'Snowbank', *Aster novae-angliae* 'Purple Dome'

Solidago rugosa 'Fireworks'
FIREWORKS GOLDENROD

Plant type: Perennial, shrublike   **Zone:** 4–8

Flower: 18-inch long sprays of bright yellow flowers give the impression of fireworks

Foliage: Fine-textured leaves on thin woody stems arch fountainlike

Bloom length: 6-plus weeks

Height: 36–40 inches   **Width/spacing:** 36 inches

Light: Full sun   **Soil:** Average, well-drained

Care: Easy; could be left up over winter for shrubby interest

Uses: Late bloomer, long bloomer, prairie, cottage garden, mid-border

Propagation: Division in spring; stem cuttings

Problems: None; does not seem to have foliar diseases seen in other golden-rods

Insider's tips: This outstanding new selection of goldenrod is the most trouble-free I have grown. The fireworks habit adds great texture and color late in the season.

Combines with: *Aconitum carmichaelii*, *Aster novae-angliae* 'Purple Dome', *Boltonia asteroides*, *Panicum virgatum* 'Rotstrahlbusch'

Sporobolus heterolepsis
PRAIRIE DROPSEED

Plant type:	Ornamental grass, native **Zone:** 3–8
Flower:	Sprays of tiny, creamy puffs
Foliage:	Slender green leaves turn golden brown and have a fountainlike shape
Bloom length:	8-plus weeks
Height:	30 inches **Width/spacing:** 30 inches
Light:	Full sun **Soil:** Average, well-drained
Care:	Cut back in late winter
Uses:	Winter interest, fragrance, prairie, edger
Propagation:	Division in spring
Problems:	None
Insider's tips:	Children will love this plant once they find out that when it blooms it smells like buttered popcorn.
Combines with:	*Tanacetum parthenium* 'Aureum', *Echinacea purpurea* 'White Swan', *Rudbeckia fulgida* var. *sullivantii* 'Goldsturm', *Solidago rugosa* 'Fireworks', *Aster novae-angliae* 'Purple Dome'

CHAPTER 7

September

*Back-to-School:
Learn to Extend
the Bloom into Fall*

Aconitum carmichaelii
FALL MONKSHOOD

Plant type:	Perennial **Zone:** 3–8
Flower:	Deep violet-blue hooded florets form spikes (sometimes give the impression of delphinium)
Foliage:	Dark green, divided clump-forming foliage with tall spiky stems
Bloom length:	7–8 weeks **Height:** 5–6 feet **Width/spacing:** 18 inches
Light:	Part shade to sun (if soil is consistently moist)
Soil:	Rich, moist, well-drained
Care:	Likes extra fertilizer
Uses:	Architectural accent, blue garden, back of the border, cut flower
Propagation:	Sow from seed and division
Problems:	Needs staking
Insider's tips:	All plant parts are poisonous if eaten! The impressive violet-blue flowers last well into November in a good year and look great with fall foliage of yellow, gold, and orange.
Combines with:	*Aster novae-angliae* 'Purple Dome', *Anemone* x *hybrida* 'Honorine Jobert', *Actaea rubra*, *Cimicifuga ramosa* 'Atropurpurea', *Miscanthus sinensis* 'Malepartus'

Anemone x *hybrida* 'Honorine Jobert'
HONORINE JOBERT JAPANESE ANEMONE

Plant type:	Perennial **Zone:** 5–7
Flower:	White, poppylike
Foliage:	Grapelike leaves in mounds
Bloom length:	4–6 weeks
Height:	3–4 feet **Width/spacing:** 36 inches
Light:	Part shade to sun **Soil:** Rich, moist, well-drained
Care:	Easy
Uses:	Mixed border, late-season bloom, white garden, cut flower
Propagation:	Division in spring
Problems:	Needs lots of space over time
Insider's tips:	'Honorine Jobert' is the most popular white-flowered, fall anemone. It was discovered in 1858.
Combines with:	*Echinacea purpurea* 'Magnus', *Aster novae-angliae* 'Alma Potschke', *Aconitum carmichaelii, Calamogrostis bracytricha*

Aster lateriflorus 'Horizontalis'
CALICO ASTER

Plant type: Perennial **Zone:** 4–7

Flower: Tiny white daisies with rosy centers (stamens) that bloom all along the stems

Foliage: Upright with dense horizontal branching, foliage becomes coppery-purple at bloom time

Bloom length: 6–8 weeks

Height: 24 inches **Width/spacing:** 12–18 inches

Light: Full sun **Soil:** Average, well-drained

Care: Easy

Uses: Textural contrast, fall color, mid-border, attracts butterflies

Propagation: Division in spring

Problems: Watch for rabbit-browse

Insider's tips: Profuse tiny blooms and contrasting dark foliage color make this aster appear to be calico. The newer selection 'Prince' has darker purple foliage.

Combines with: *Sedum* x 'Autumn Joy', *Veronica alpina* 'Goodness Grows', *Hemerocallis* 'Happy Returns', *Campanula carpatica* 'Deep Blue Clips'

Aster novae-angliae 'Alma Potschke'
ALMA POTSCHKE NEW ENGLAND ASTER

Plant type:	Perennial **Zone:** 4–8
Flower:	Raspberry-pink, 1-inch daisies
Foliage:	Tall stems become floppier as plant blooms
Bloom length:	5–6 weeks
Height:	3–4 feet **Width/spacing:** 3 feet
Light:	Full sun **Soil:** Average, well-drained
Care:	Cut back by half in early summer for shorter, denser habit
Uses:	Bright fall color, accent, cottage garden, prairie/meadow
Propagation:	Division in spring; remove declining center
Problems:	Powdery mildew; topples from weight of profuse blooms; not easily staked
Insider's tips:	Although this aster is very floppy, the color is so outstanding that I try to use other plants to help hold it up. The best I have found so far is the shrub crimson barberry.
Combines with:	*Rudbeckia triloba, Caryopteris* x *clandonensis* 'Longwood Blue', *Boltonia asteroides, Solidago rugosa* 'Fireworks', *Veronica spicata* 'Blue Charm'

Aster novae-angliae 'Purple Dome'
NEW ENGLAND ASTER

Plant type: Perennial   **Zone:** 3–8

Flower: Purple, 1-inch daisies cover the plant, forming a dome

Foliage: Compact, mounded and clump-forming

Bloom length: 6–8 weeks

Height: 24 inches   **Width/spacing:** 24 inches

Light: Sun to light shade   **Soil:** Average, well-drained

Care: Deadhead to prevent seedlings, which do not come true to form

Uses: Edger, border, formal garden, fall color, attracts butterflies

Propagation: Division in spring; will have many offshoots

Problems: Rabbits love to browse all asters

Insider's tips: Asters that do not flop are a priority in my garden. I get my asters to be more tightly compacted by shearing them in early June. Foliar diseases are less troublesome for 'Purple Dome' than for other asters, but they occasionally occur in hot, humid, and wet summers.

Combines with: *Rosa* 'Betty Prior', *Hemerocallis* 'Happy Returns', *Sedum* x 'Autumn Joy', *Anaphalis triplinervis, Anemone* x *hybrida* 'Honorine Jobert'

Calamogrostis bracytricha
FEATHER GRASS

Plant type:	Ornamental grass **Zone:** 4–9
Flower:	Fluffy foxtail starts as green with a hint of pink, turning a light tan
Foliage:	More cascading clump than feather reed grass
Bloom length:	6-plus weeks
Height:	3–5 feet **Width/spacing:** 3 feet
Light:	Part shade to sun **Soil:** Average to rich, evenly moist
Care:	Cut back in late winter (early April in the Midwest)
Uses:	Architectural accent, screening, winter interest, mixed border, woodland edge
Propagation:	Division in spring
Problems:	None
Insider's tips:	Finally, a nice architectural grass for the shadier site!
Combines with:	*Rudbeckia fulgida* var. *sullivantii* 'Goldsturm', *Eupatorium coelestinum*, *Echinacea purpurea* 'Magnus', *Sedum* x 'Autumn Joy'

CHAPTER 8

October

*It's No Trick —
These Glorious Grasses
and Late Bloomers
Are a Real Treat!*

Cimicifuga simplex 'White Pearl'
WHITE PEARL KAMCHATKA BUGBANE

Plant type:	Perennial **Zone:** 3–7
Flower:	Fragrant, bright white, dense, 2-inch spikes presented on wandlike stems
Foliage:	Looks like a loose astilbe
Bloom length:	4–6 weeks, dependent on frost
Height:	3–4 feet **Width/spacing:** 30 inches
Light:	Part shade, shade **Soil:** Average to rich, evenly moist
Care:	Easy
Uses:	Architectural accent, late bloomer, fragrance
Propagation:	Deep root system does not divide easily
Problems:	Slow to mature
Insider's tips:	This late bloomer is refreshingly welcome in the late season garden. By mixing these with *Cimicifuga racemosa* and *Cimicifuga ramosa* 'Hillside Black Beauty' or 'Atropurpurea', you can have wands of white from July to November.
Combines with:	*Cimicifuga racemosa*, *Cimicifuga ramosa* 'Hillside Black Beauty' or 'Atropurpurea', *Amsonia tabernaemontana*, *Onoclea sensibilis*, *Hosta* 'Piedmont Gold'

Miscanthus sinensis 'Morning Light'
MORNING LIGHT VARIEGATED MAIDEN GRASS

Plant type: Ornamental grass **Zone:** 5–9

Flower: Bronze-red plume ages to wheat

Foliage: Silver-striped, green, very narrow leaves give the appearance of a pale, gray fountain

Bloom length: 6 weeks

Height: 4–5 feet **Width/spacing:** 4 feet

Light: Sun to light shade **Soil:** Average to rich, evenly moist

Care: Cut down in late winter before new growth appears

Uses: Massing, foliage color and texture, architectural accent, winter interest

Propagation: Division after cutting back in late winter—a heavy-duty job!

Problems: Blooms so late in the North that it is often stunted by frosts

Insider's tips: This maiden grass blooms so late that frosts may ruin the inflorescence. This is a really silvery-gray grass throughout the season, but when photographed in the late autumn it appears golden from the reflected fall light.

Combines with: *Sedum* x 'Autumn Joy', *Heliopsis helianthoides* 'Summer Sun', *Aster* x *frikartii* 'Monch', *Aster novae-angliae* 'Alma Potschke', other ornamental grasses

Miscanthus sinensis 'Strictus'
ZEBRA GRASS

Plant type: Ornamental grass   **Zone:** 5–9

Flower: Reddish-brown plume turns beige in winter

Foliage: Showy, yellow, vertical zebra stripes on arching grasslike leaves

Bloom length: 4-plus weeks

Height: 5–6 feet   **Width/spacing:** 5 feet

Light: Full sun   **Soil:** Average to rich, evenly moist

Care: Cut to about 2 inches in late winter before new growth begins

Uses: Background, new American garden, mixed border, architectural accent

Propagation: Division after cutting down

Problems: None

Insider's tips: This selection of zebra grass is the hardiest for Zone 5. Watch for shorter forms with yellow zebra stripes.

Combines with: *Solidago rugosa* 'Fireworks', *Boltonia asteroides*, *Rudbeckia nitida* 'Herbstsonne', *Eupatorium maculatum* 'Gateway', *Helenium autumnale*

Tricyrtis hirta 'Miyazaki'
TOAD LILY

Plant type:	Perennial **Zone:** 5–8
Flower:	Pinkish-white with darker spots, flowers look like miniature orchids
Foliage:	Arching stems with flowers growing out of the alternating leaf axils
Bloom length:	4–6 weeks
Height:	24–30 inches **Width/spacing:** 24 inches
Light:	Part shade, shade **Soil:** Rich, moist
Care:	Easy
Uses:	Collector's plant, unusual form, late bloomer, shade garden
Propagation:	Division in early spring while dormant
Problems:	Blooms so late
Insider's tips:	This plant blooms so late in a shaded site that many gardeners miss seeing it bloom! Sprays of miniature orchids hang on through some of the coldest weather.
Combines with:	*Helleborus orientalis, Vinca minor, Polystichum acrostichoides, Dryopteris marginalis, Hakonechloa macra* 'Aureola'

What's Still Blooming?

In October, over forty-five perennials are still in bloom in the "continuous bloom" garden! Record how many are still in bloom in your garden so you can plan for next fall. And be prepared to have your neighbors ask how you created such a beautiful, colorful garden while their gardens have nothing but dried-up stems! (Note: * indicates perennials that sometimes will extend their bloom time or repeat bloom later in the season.)

Aconitum carmichaelii

Anaphalis triplinervis 'Summer Snow'*
   (August–September)

*Anemone sylvestris** (May–June)

Anemone x *hybrida* 'Honorine Jobert'

Anemone vitifolia 'Robustissima'

Aster divaricatus

Aster x *frikartii* 'Monch'* (July–September)

Aster lateriflorus 'Horizontalis'

Aster novae-angliae 'Alma Potschke'

Aster novae-angliae 'Purple Dome'

*Bergenia cordifolia** (April–May)

Boltonia asteroides 'Snowbank'

Calamagrostis x *acutiflora* 'Karl Foerster'

Calamagrostis bracytricha

Ceratostigma plumbaginoides

*Chelone lyonii** (August–September)

Cimicifuga simplex 'White Pearl'

Coreopsis verticillata 'Moonbeam'

Corydalis lutea

Eupatorium coelestinum

Eupatorium rugosum 'Chocolate'

Gaura lindheimeri

Gaura lindheimeri 'Siskiyou Pink'

Geranium sanguineum var. *striatum** (May–August)

Geranium wallichianum 'Buxton's Variety'

Hemerocallis 'Happy Returns'

Hemerocallis 'Stella d'Oro'

Miscanthus sinensis 'Kaskade'

Miscanthus sinensis 'Malepartus'

Miscanthus sinensis 'Morning Light'

Miscanthus sinensis 'Nippon'

Miscanthus sinensis 'Purpurescens'

Miscanthus sinensis 'Strictus'

Nepeta mussinii 'Blue Wonder'

Panicum virgatum 'Rotstrahlbusch'

*Patrinia scabiosifolia** (August–September)

Pennisetum alopecuroides

Phlox paniculata 'David'* (July–September)

Phlox paniculata 'Eva Cullum'* (July–September)

Physostegia virginiana 'Vivid'* (August–September)

Rosa 'Betty Prior'

Rosa 'Carefree Delight'

Rosa 'Carefree Wonder'

Rosa 'Flower Carpet'

Rosa 'Knock Out'

Rosa 'Showbiz'

Rudbeckia nitida 'Herbstsonne'* (July–September)

Salvia x *superba* 'Blue Hill'

Salvia x *superba* 'May Night'

Scabiosa columbaria 'Butterfly Blue'

Sedum x 'Autumn Joy'

Solidago rugosa 'Fireworks'

Sporobolus heterolepsis

Tricyrtis hirta 'Miyazaki'

Veronica alpina 'Goodness Grows'

November

The Last Hurrah!

Getting the Garden Ready for Winter

Like anything else, the best way to prepare your garden for the winter is to *plan* the work ahead of time. With some forethought, you won't be racing around your yard right before Thanksgiving trying to get all the work done before your family arrives from out of town.

The garden work you do now will pay a myriad of dividends for each succeeding season. In the fall, you prepare your winter-tidy garden. This cuts down time you would spend in the spring opening your garden. Finally, mulching now improves soil fertility and moisture retention for the summer. A little maintenance now will allow you to enjoy the beginning of a long season of bloom next spring.

Water as necessary until Thanksgiving

The weather has cooled off, but that's no reason to think that your garden doesn't need the water it did in August. Continue to water throughout fall if rain is insufficient. Plants need about one inch per week, regardless of temperature. Check dry areas under maple trees, too. Remember that herbaceous plants die back to the ground only—the roots are still living!

Cutting the garden down

After each cold spell throughout the fall, you will notice that perennials gradually yellow, then brown, and lose their leaves. Cutting down each group of plants as they go dormant saves you from the one-day whirlwind effort to cut down your whole garden. Think of this as an end-of-the-season housecleaning done in *stages*.

Generally, cut each plant down to its basal clump of leaves, getting rid of any dead plant material that could encourage garden pests to overwinter. Disease-free plant material can be chopped up and mixed into your compost pile. Plants such as Shasta daisies will especially benefit from this cutting back as well as from an extra firming of the soil around the roots to keep them from frost-heaving. Take extra care with *Aster frikartii* 'Monch' and *Scabiosa columbaria* 'Butterfly Blue', which need mulching in northern zones to winter over. (And even then I occasionally lose some.)

If you have annuals in your garden, removing them now will save you work in the spring. And remember to sprinkle any seeds of alyssum, cleome, or larkspur where you want them for next year.

Maintaining roses

Maintenance of roses is done in November after a hard frost. Roses need to be mounded as high as possible with potting soil (I use half of a 40-pound bag), finished compost, and ground up leaves or sawdust. Remove all rose leaves that will be covered, especially those showing black spot. The purpose of this mounding is to keep the crown and roots well frozen throughout the winter. No rose cones, please, as this only heats up the plants on really warm winter days and encourages disease. Do not cut back rose canes until spring.

Mine That Gold!

Instead of bagging those fall leaves and sending them off for recycling, use that nutritional "gold mine" to sheet compost all of your garden beds over winter. Think of this as part of nature's process of decomposition for renewal—remember, there is no "blow-and-mow" crew in the forest! By mowing twice, once without the mower bag and once with it for collecting, leaves will be finely ground and will decompose rapidly. You should save this "gold" until your beds are tidied and the ground is beginning to freeze, usually around Thanksgiving. Put the leaf mulch onto all gardens at least 3 inches deep, but not on top of the plants left up over the winter.

This simple and cost-efficient job serves two important purposes: 1) The decomposing leaf mold improves the tilth, opening clay soils and adding humus to sandy soils. 2) The leaf mold breaks down to become nutrient-rich humus, increasing the fertility of depleted soil. This top-down method of soil improvement emulates nature again, as worms, rain, and snow work the mulch into the soil and improves it over the winter.

There is no need to dig the mulch into the existing soil layer. Half of it will decompose by spring, and the rest can remain undisturbed to become a summer mulch and a weed suppressant. And don't worry about your up-coming plants—perennials and bulbs easily push through the decomposing "leaf mold" in the spring.

Achieving Winter Color and Interest

OK, perennials aren't actively growing in the winter, but who says they can't spice up your bleak winter landscape? Many of the perennials in this book had "winter interest" listed in their uses in the garden. They can achieve that interest if they're left "up" throughout the winter. Maybe they're evergreen. Maybe the foliage offers color or unique shape. Maybe the seed heads will make people do a double take as they drive by. And these patterns or textures will only improve as snow and ice cover them after a storm.

The following easy-access lists should help you plan your winter garden. Plants in the first list, evergreen perennials, should not be cut back during winter bed preparation. Instead, you'll want to cut off winterkill in the spring. Plants in the second list will have interesting foliage or seed heads. Perennials marked with a star (*) may be cut down if you do not want the added benefit these plants provide. And beware: *Rudbeckia fulgida* var. *sullivantii* 'Goldsturm' reseeds itself like crazy, so decide now if you can live with the multitude of seedlings the winter interest will produce next spring.

Evergreen perennials

Arabis caucasica 'Snowcap' (gray-green)
Asarum europaeum
Bergenia cordifolia
Dianthus x *allwoodii* 'Doris' (gray-blue)
Dryopteris marginalis
Epimedium 'Crimson'
Helictotrichon sempervirens (chalky blue)
Helleborus orientalis
Heuchera 'Plum Pudding' (burgundy)
Iberis sempervirens 'Purity'
Iris tectorum

Lamium maculatum 'White Nancy' (silvery white)
Lavandula angustifolia 'Hidcote' (silver-gray)
Phlox stolonifera
Polystichum acrostichoides
Tiarella wherryi
Veronica 'Minuet' (silver-gray)

Perennials for foliage or seed heads

Artemisia stelleriana 'Silver Brocade'
Asclepias tuberosa
Astilbe cultivars—for their seed heads
Calamagrostis bracytricha
Calamagrostis x *acutiflora* 'Karl Foerster'
Carex elata 'Bowles Golden'*
Coreopsis verticillata 'Moonbeam'
Echinacea purpurea 'Magnus'
Echinacea purpurea 'White Swan'
Eryngium yuccifolium
Hakonechloa macra 'Aureola'*
Iris sibirica 'Caesar's Brother'*
Miscanthus sinensis cultivars
Origanum vulgare 'Aureum'
Panicum virgatum 'Rotstrahlbusch'
Pennisetum alopecuroides
Perovskia atriplicifolia
Rosa cultivars—for the rose hips
Rudbeckia fulgida var. *sullivantii* 'Goldsturm'
Sedum x 'Autumn Joy'
Sorghastrum nutans 'Sioux Blue'
Sporobolus heterolepsis
Stachys byzantina

Interplanting Bulbs in the Perennial Garden

As a general rule of thumb, you should plant bulbs at a depth three times the height of bulb—except for tulips, which will perennialize better from an eight-inch depth. And good drainage is an absolute *must,* as bulbs rot in standing water any time of the year!

To extend the bloom season for the "continuous bloom" garden, gardeners will need to interplant bulbs in the perennial garden in fall. Instead of planting bulbs one-by-one and trailing them through the garden, I recommend a cluster planting technique started by my sister over twenty years ago. In between perennials, dig holes 12 inches in diameter and 8 to 10 inches deep. Space five tulip or five daffodil bulbs equidistantly around the bottom edge of the hole. Sprinkle a handful of Bulb Booster in the hole, then crumble soil over the bulbs until hole is filled to two inches from the top. If soil is poor, add finished compost and mix with existing soil to fill. In the top two inches, space five grape hyacinth bulbs between the bulbs already planted and fill with remaining soil, tamping to firm. When finished, water the planting beds with a sprinkler for about an hour. This will settle the soil around the bulbs and encourage new root development. Continue to water if rainfall is insufficient.

The results in spring will be bouquets or clusters of ten plants with combinations of violet-blue grape hyacinths, green foliage, and yellow, pink, red, or white tulips or daffodils. The advantages to this technique are: It's easier to plant ten bulbs at once rather than on at a time, and it avoids the "soldiers lined in a row" look or "snakes" of plants running through the garden. There is one last reason to use this cluster planting technique.

Early in the fall, grape hyacinth leaves reappear, marking the area where bulbs were planted in previous years. This saves you the headache—and maybe even heartache—of accidentally digging up existing bulb plantings.

Experience has shown that first-time bulb gardeners are disappointed if they order less than a hundred daffodil or tulip bulbs (that's just twenty holes to dig!). When you order one hundred daffodils or tulips, you will also need to order one hundred grape hyacinth. It is also best to dig all the holes in the garden first so you don't forget and dig up bulbs you've already planted.

For planting bulbs other than tulips and daffodils, dig holes to accommodate three bulbs. Add Bulb Booster and crumbled soil, then water. Siberian squill, aconites, snowdrops, windflowers, summer snowflakes, ornamental onions, camass, and lilies do not need grape hyacinth markers.

As for animals in the garden, daffodils, grape hyacinth, and blue scillas are not bothered by rodents or deer. If squirrels and chipmunks ravage your tulip beds, sprinkle the holes with crushed mothballs or F&B Dog and Rabbit Repellent.

Winter

Who Stops Gardening in Winter?

Armchair Gardening

What do true gardeners do during winter? They imagine how glorious their garden will be next summer, and they spend a lot of time planning how to make that happen!

Starting before Christmas, catalogs from nurseries and seed companies begin filling mailboxes—my Thompson & Morgan catalog arrived before Thanksgiving. I find I just can't wait to see what is new, either with better bloom, new flower and foliage color, or improved and unusual form. Then I check to see if any of the "in" plants have come down in price from the previous year.

The picture catalogs are particularly enticing because of the color pictures of flowers and foliage and because of their good ideas about combinations. Wayside Gardens and White Flower Farm are great examples of catalogs I like—they have exciting new plant offerings and so much for your eyes to feast on. I also like to *read* White Flower's catalog because of all the helpful information about plant habit and cultivation written over the years by Amos Pettingill. Another highly visual catalog is Shady Oaks Nursery; its emphasis is on shade-tolerant plants and includes spectacular pictures of hostas by Clayton Oslund. This catalog could easily serve as a hosta resource guide to help you sort out the many new cultivars, and it is the only catalog where I have found a favorite woodland native rue anemone, *Anemonella thalictroides.*

The "no picture" catalogs tend to be for the plant connoisseur. Tiny details in the written description can be just what the "plant nut" is looking for to add to his/her collection. And there seem to be a plethora of choices within genera carried by each nursery. I find, too, that these catalogs also talk about hardiness and habitat experiences, particularly with the new and unusual plant materials.

My favorite catalogs tend to be those that are fun to read because the writer has a good sense of humor or gives really practical advice. Take a look at Plant Delights Nursery, Arrowhead Alpines, and Heronswood Nursery, each having individualized descriptions of plants as well as some choice hard-to-

find plants. Look for *Delphinium* 'Duncan McGlashan Hybrids' at Arrowhead Alpines, and how can you resist a perennial bachelor button called *Centaurea montana* 'Presley's Blue Hawaii'? Tony Avent's catalog, Plant Delights Nursery Inc., is a real hoot to read—just imagine what you will find in a catalog priced at ten stamps or a box of chocolates and announces "Warning: The Horticulture General has determined that opening this catalog may cause mental impairment and intoxication". He carries many of the new jewel-toned lobelias and something called Chocolate Flower, *Berlandiera lyrata.* This year I will have my order in early to Heronswood Nursery for *Geranium wallichianum* 'Buxton's Variety', a low-growing perennial geranium with blue flowers and white centers that blooms into September.

There are, of course, specialty nurseries for every kind of plant—roses, geraniums, rhododendrons, irises, daylilies, and peonies, for example. If you are a collector, you have already discovered your favorites. Then there are catalogs for the prairie (Prairie Nursery), the collector (Collector's Nursery, Roslyn Nursery, and Siskiyou Rare Plant Nursery), and those who are on a tight budget and looking for "tried and true" plants (Bluestone Perennials). I use the white false indigo from Prairie Nursery and have had good luck with blue-flowered *Corydalis elata* from Collector's Nursery.

And finally, I cherish catalogs that tell you how wide the plant will grow! Milaeger's in Racine, Wisconsin, was the first to provide this helpful information and has an incredible, ever-increasing variety of perennials each year. In 1999, Milaeger's didn't produce their usual color catalog but published it online at www.garden.com. This is where I have gotten my favorite dwarf balloon flower, *Platycodon grandiflorus* 'Sentimental Blue' and the shade-tolerant golden grass, *Carex elata* 'Bowles Golden'.

Gardening from seed adds a whole other dimension to armchair gardening by allowing you to be involved with the life cycle of a plant. This is also a great opportunity to get your hands on plants that you can't find locally because they can *only* be purchased as seed. Starting plants from seed, while time consuming, is not terribly difficult and has proved worth it for those who raise their own vegetables or unusual annuals and perennials. Helpful catalogs for starting plants from seed are Thompson & Morgan, W. Atlee Burpee, Mellinger's, and Gardener's Supply. All have supplies and information on starting plants from seed.

Good sources for other catalogs can be found in the advertisement or index section of garden magazines. And you'll find a list of catalogs I use in appendix F of this book.

Which brings me to how I spend much of my time in winter snuggled up near the fireplace, reading all the magazines and books I had no time for during gardening season. Besides seeing and reading about wonderful plants and gardens, you will get great ideas on what to do (design) and how to do it (cultivation).

Now the problem comes if you do not have a photographic memory and have not bothered to make notes on what ideas or plants you wish to try. A small "sticky notepad" and pencil sit on top of my basket of catalogs, magazines, and books so that I can use them as bookmark reminders with annotations of things that have caught my fancy and are important to remember. With this part completed, you are ready to take the next step in armchair gardening—planning.

Unfortunately for most of us, we must now figure out where we will plant all our new dreams or where we can possibly fit in the plants that we just have to try. Speaking from experience, it does not work to just order hundreds of dollars worth of plants with the hope that space in your garden will miraculously open up on the day of the UPS delivery!

It helps tremendously to have snapshots of all of your garden spaces throughout the gardening season. Without these, you must try to visualize where there were holes in the garden or where you could remove plants that no longer please you because of their habit or appropriateness to your garden. Simply reducing the spread of some plants may create the much-needed space for new treasures.

Photos of your garden will help with more than just fitting in new plants. By taking pictures each season—even in winter—you keep a visual record of your successes so you can repeat them and of your failures so you can avoid them in the future. During each season, take pictures before and after installation and before and after any major changes to your gardens. And make sure you take shots of the whole garden, not just close-ups of each plant. You'll be able to see combinations that worked well and any problems plants had, such as pest damage or being in the wrong site. Also important, over the years you'll see the progress that not only your garden has made, but also that you've made as a gardener!

Evaluating and Planning as Part of the Gardening Process

When planning for next year's garden, it doesn't matter which tools you use . . . as long as they help you. Photos and sketches on graph paper may be your preferred method, or maybe you use the latest landscaping CD-ROMs on the market. If it helps you to have a beautiful garden, keep doing it. The important thing is to have a plan of attack and get it on paper—or on screen—*now*, before you forget the dream of next summer's garden.

The following outline should help you evaluate how your garden performed over the last season and then plan your changes for next year.

I. Evaluate: What Happened in Your Garden This Year?
   A. Which plants have flopped? Are any invasive?
   B. Are plants the right plant in the right place?
   C. Are you happy with what you see?
   D. Is it time to enlarge your garden space?
   E. Does your soil appear a little "lean" or compacted?
II. Plan: What's Happening in Your Garden Right Now?
   A. What should I do throughout the fall?
      1. Water
      2. Weed and remove dead plant material
      3. Continue to deadhead for repeat bloom and to keep some plants from reseeding (rudbeckia and allium)

4. Add fall-blooming plants: mums, asters, and/or grasses
5. Make sure your reseeding annuals are seeded where you need the color; collect and distribute the seed

B. In the winter?
   1. What is currently providing winter interest or color?
   2. What can be added for interest next winter?

C. For next spring?
   1. Do you have spring-flowering bulbs?
   2. Are your bulbs putting on less of a show each year? If bulbs are blooming less:
      a. Bulbs were not planted deeply enough
      b. Help older bulbs by adding a handful of Bulb Booster in the spring to feed the bulb for next year's blooms

3. Do you get impatient waiting for bulb foliage to ripen? If you really hate ugly, ripening foliage:
   a. Don't plant bulbs!
   b. Cut the entire plant down when it's finished blooming. Of course, you will need to plant new bulbs each year because all bulbs need the leaves to "manufacture food" in order to produce flowers in coming years.

With the answers to these questions, you can begin planning for the next year's growing season.

Tips

Nitty-Gritty Tips for Good Garden Care

Gardens are meant to be enjoyed. You, your family, neighbors, and passersby will enjoy the colors, textures, scents, and wildlife the flowers attract. And you should enjoy the time spent tending your garden. If you're not, you're probably missing the point. Gardening should be therapeutic, relaxing, invigorating, not a chore you need to perform each week.

This chapter will help you enjoy the process of gardening by showing you some shortcuts and tips I've picked up over the years and by explaining many of the terms you may hear in your garden center or on HGTV. It's my hope that you will enjoy gardening as much as I do.

The Fifteen-Minute Garden Solution

I like to ask gardeners and students who participate in my garden workshops to plan on spending only fifteen minutes each day in their garden with a cup of coffee or tea in the morning or a glass of wine in late afternoon. This is your time to enjoy the daily changes in your garden and to determine if there are any problems. And it eliminates the "chore" of spending an entire day on the weekend maintaining the garden.

By using this small amount of time daily to walk about and check your garden, you can readily pull weeds in their early stage of growth and spot bugs and diseases before they become rampant. This daily perusal assures that you are on top of any problems, and soon you will become familiar with how nature works and will be taking part in a helpful and pleasurable management program. At the end of the week you will have worked to maintain your garden 1¾ hours and will have smelled the flowers and felt the sense of accomplishment in helping the garden to grow successfully!

And if you spent more than fifteen minutes a day in your garden? *Good for you!* You are well on your way to becoming a true gardener. And your beautiful garden is the reward.

Tidy gardens always look good and don't breed problems. By using the fifteen-minute program, the following maintenance steps will be a piece of cake!

1. Weed! Pull or dig out anything that competes with your garden plants, especially grass. The sooner this is done, the easier it is to do, as you'll never have a lot to do at one time. Weeding right after a rain is best; the weeds pull out with a minimum of effort.
2. Remove dead or diseased plant parts as you notice them.
3. Deadhead spent flowers—this encourages continued bloom and keeps the garden looking fresh.
4. Stake plants if necessary, or use varieties that don't need staking.

Basic Perennial Planting Tips

Here are a few ideas that will make your initial planting easier. With a little forethought, you'll be able to plant in an organized and efficient manner, leaving more time for you and your family to enjoy the garden.

1. Plant after *all* perennials have been collected, not as you get them. Remember to water plants while you wait to plant them all.
2. Layout your plants before digging. Stand back to view the arrangement, shifting plants as necessary.
3. Plant from the back of the garden to the front. Or for an island planting, plant from the center outward.
4. Do not plant when soil is overly wet. Soil should crumble easily in your hand.
5. Be careful to *not* compact soil by stepping on it unnecessarily. Soil should be as loose and airy as possible.
6. Remember to plan for access and add steppers for maintaining your garden.

Planting Guide

You'd think it'd be as simple as digging a hole and dropping the plant in, right? While that's the basic idea, a few extra steps will help the plants establish themselves more quickly and more vigorously.

1. Water pots before planting.
2. Prepare a 50/50 mixture of soil and organic matter, such as composted manure, mushroom compost, or homemade finished compost from the garden.

3. Dig a hole for the plant, allowing space at the bottom and side for organic mixture. A drain spade or post-hole digger works great for 1-gallon pots.

4. Place organic mixture in the hole, working it into the soil at the bottom with a spading fork or drain spade.

5. Tap the plant out of the container and pull the roots into a downward position, especially if the plant is pot-bound. If extremely pot-bound, use pruners to cut and untangle roots as necessary. Loosing some roots to do this is OK; your plant will be better off in the long run.

6. Set the plant at the same depth that it was growing at when it was in the container, directing the roots out and down. Add or remove compost as necessary.

7. Fill in around the root ball with compost using your hands to push it in well so that there are no air pockets. Press more compost around top of plant to firm it into position.

8. Water thoroughly, allowing soil and compost to settle down around the root ball. Add soil and compost if necessary to keep root ball level with the surrounding bed.

9. Do not fertilize. The compost you added to the existing soil supplies all the necessary nutrients. Fertilizing only stresses the plant, which needs to focus its energy on establishing itself.

Soil Tips: Getting Down and Dirty

Remember that good soil produces good roots. And good soil is airy and full of nutrients. To open soil that has become compacted, push a spading fork as deeply as possible into the soil, then rock it back and forth. This helps air and water flow through the soil to the plant's roots. Do not turn the soil, as this only brings weed seeds to the light. The ideal soil is a rich, dark, crumbly loam that goes at least 12 inches deep. The soil should be made up of about 25 percent water, 50 percent solid particles (45 percent minerals and 5 percent organics), and 25 percent air.

Composting

The best all-around soil amendment is compost. When you amend the soil, you improve its texture. And improving the texture will provide three main benefits: It will increase soil porosity, allowing for percolation of air and water; it will increase water retention; and it creates a microclimate for beneficial soil organisms, including worms.

I find the best application is by sheet composting, which means covering the garden with a "sheet" of compost. Around Thanksgiving, after your final bed "cut down," apply twice-ground leaves 3 to 6 inches deep over beds. In the spring, sheet compost again with finished garden compost, mushroom compost, or composted manure.

Fertilizing

In addition to compost, you need to fertilize your garden beds. You'll want to do this three times over the season—once in early May, again in early June, and the last time in early August. Never apply fertilizer after August 16. Fertilizing in late summer or fall will stimulate new growth, which is likely to kill perennials going dormant.

But what to use? I think solid organic fertilizers such as New Jersey green sand, pelletized chicken manure, and composted manure are best because they can add grit to the soil. Other organic fertilizers can be used while watering, such as liquid seaweed and fish emulsion.

Mulching

Mulching is the key to reducing garden maintenance. It reduces the need for water and cuts down on weed germination. Several different mulches are available, and it's your choice as to which you want to use. You can choose from finished compost (homemade, composted manure, or mushroom compost), nut or cocoa shells, shredded dried leaves, or grass clippings—but do not allow clippings to mat!

Watering

Watering is critical for every garden. Why? Because plants are 90 percent water, and they'll use one hundred times their weight in water. Water is important in feeding plants, as minerals that have been dissolved in water are carried up to the plants by their root hairs. And lastly, plants cool themselves by evaporating water.

Over the first few weeks, make sure new plantings stay watered. Do not allow them to dehydrate. Use a soaker hose or a sprinkler. Please resist the urge to water by hand, which usually results in an inadequate watering of only the top of the soil. The best time to water is before noon. Water each location for at least one hour, as deep watering develops a large, deep root system and determines the quality of the plant you actually see.

New Garden Soil Preparation

The easiest way to start a new garden from scratch is something I call the raised-bed method. The idea is to add organic material in layers on top of existing soil without the backbreaking job of cultivating and turning the soil.

Fall

The best time to prepare new garden beds is in the fall. Preparing them before winter lets the materials break down over several months' time, feeding the soil naturally and inexpensively.

If your soil has 6 inches of dark loam, use a spading fork or rocker tool to loosen and open up subsoil. Add a 6-inch-deep layer mown leaves and grass clippings sprinkled with fertilizer to aid breakdown. Adding chicken manure speeds decomposition. Then allow the bed to "cook" over winter.

If your soil is mostly compacted clay, spade the soil and leave it rough, which will allow the freezes and thaws to break up the clumps over the course of the winter. Add an 8-to-12-inch-deep mixture of equal parts of topsoil and leaf or grass clippings with fertilizer or topsoil and finished compost (8 to 12 inches). Allow the bed to cook over winter. I think it's important to say here that clay soils are not all bad! The very fine particles absorb and retain water. Also, these particles have much-needed minerals and are more easily carried by water to the plants. So don't despair if you live in a region with clay soil.

If your soil is very sandy, follow the method above but without spading the ground.

You may wish to use a weed barrier of several layers of newspaper between the soil and leaf/grass layer. Even if newspaper does not fully breakdown, you can cut through it to plant in the spring. Gardeners often use this technique to shade out existing sod or rhizomatous plants. I would also use a good sprinkling of fertilizer on undesirable plants to "burn" them out.

Spring or early summer

New garden beds prepared in spring can be more costly because you may need to buy the composted materials, and the advantages of using nature to break up compacted soil over the winter are lost. If rototilling is the only option, wait until soils have dried out from the spring rains. Rototilling wet soil will change the soil structure and will lead to even further soil compaction.

Roses

Roses are a very important part of the "continuous bloom" perennial garden. Starting in June, many rose bushes burst into bloom and repeat until frost. It is the gardener's job to know which roses work best in their climate and to wisely choose the ones with the most disease resistance and the longest repeat bloom.

Basic rose care

In the spring after new growth has appeared on your roses, the potting soil or any other winter mulch may be gently pushed away from the crown or watered away with a sprinkling wand. Be particularly sure that you have waited long enough for any damaging frosts to disappear—usually late April or early May in northeastern Illinois. Check on the latest frost recorded in your region to be safe. Now you may prune out any winterkill and cut dead (non-green) stems back to fresh, new growth.

Roses do especially well with a handful of New Jersey green sand spread around each plant early May, early June, *and* in early August, before the sixteenth. Trust me on this one, as you will be astounded at how well your roses will look throughout summer. You can find New Jersey green sand at most garden centers.

Finally, if you are planting new roses this year, try sprinkling a handful of Epsom salts in the planting hole to get your roses off to a good start. This works like a mineral tonic and is not a fertilizer, which can burn new root systems.

Winter care

Preparing roses for winter is done in November, after a hard frost. You need to mound roses by pouring either potting soil (use half of a 40-pound bag), finished compost, or ground-up leaves over the crown of the plant—this makes great insulating material. Remove all rose leaves that will be covered. The purpose of this mounding is to keep the crown and roots well frozen throughout the winter! No rose cones, please, as these only heat up the plants on really warm winter days and cause fungal problems. Do not cut back rose canes until spring.

As with the entire perennial border, adequate water is important until Thanksgiving. This *usually* does not require additional watering because of the wet and rainy fall season, but please monitor how much rainfall you're getting. All plants need one inch of water per week, so be ready with the soaker hose or sprinkler.

Tips and Tools for the Allergic Gardener

My favorite tools

- Green Thumb garden gloves—flexible with a good grip for hand protection
- Drain spade—best for planting perennials. Make sure you keep it sharp!
- Weed digger or small screwdriver—for weeding as well as dividing
- Felco pruners—use #6 if you have smaller hands. The red handles don't get lost in the grass.
- Cup hooks or Ross Bird Netting for training vines
- Spading fork for opening compact soil
- Camera to record successes and mistakes

Fertilizers

- Energy Buttons, which are pelletized chicken manure
- Mushroom compost
- Composted manure
- Finished homemade compost
- New Jersey green sand, which I highly recommend for roses
- Finely ground leaves or bark mixed with composted manure—many commercial mixes are available at garden centers
- A spring tonic of Epsom salts from your local supermarket or drug store. This is an old Jerry Baker trick.

Pest control

Beneficial insects, such as ladybugs

For chewing and sucking insects

- Safer insecticidal soap with pyrethrin
- Ringer Attack
- Diazinon granules—Diazinon is a chemical, so wear gloves when applying. The granules have less risk of getting on your skin than does the spray.

For slugs

- Diatomaceous earth
- Sand or chicken grit
- Rolled-up and water-soaked newspaper
- Yeast or beer in sunken margarine tubs
- Spraying slugs with a mixture of equal parts vinegar and water—best time is after dark
- Hand-picking them—*yuck!*

For rabbits

- F&B Dog and Rabbit Repellant—do not use this around edibles. This product contains crushed mothballs and pepper. Always use gloves when applying.

- Milorganite—make a 1-inch border around garden. This is processed Milwaukee sludge. Wear gloves when applying, and do not use around edibles.

For deer

- Milorganite—make a 1-inch border around garden. This is processed Milwaukee sludge. Wear gloves when applying, and do not use around edibles.
- Deer Away powder—it's basically powdered egg solids—and it smells like rotten eggs! Should last five to six weeks.

Diseases

The trick is to spray fungicides every two weeks starting in June—or to use only disease-resistant perennials.
- SunSpray Horticultural Oil—for black spot and powdery mildew
- Safer fungicidal soap
- 1 tablespoon baking soda and 2½ tablespoons of SunSpray Horticultural Oil in 1 gallon of water

The Mystery Solved! Deadheading, Pinching, and Cutting Back

Deadheading is not some mysterious gardening lingo, or at least it shouldn't be. It simply means to remove flowers that have finished blooming. Some look like brown dried flowers, while others dangle on their stem like faded wet hankies. All detract from the colorful display of flowers you want for your garden.

Pinching refers to pinching off the growth tip and the first leaves with your thumb and forefinger to get bushier plants with more bloom. The flowers then produced will be smaller and bloom later. I actually use the term as *pinching for height control* and use pruners to cut the plant height in half in early June so that I don't have big plants flopping all over their neighbors in late summer.

Finally, some plants will benefit from *cutting back* or cutting everything to the ground after blooming to regenerate new, fresh foliage (but not flowers).

Although this sounds drastic, it works well on plants that are tired looking with floppy yellow or brown leaves.

Deadhead for repeat bloom

Aguilegia longissima 'Maxistar' (columbine)
Achillea x 'Anthea' (yarrow)
Campanula carpatica (bellflower)
Coreopsis grandiflora 'Sunray'
Coreopsis verticillata 'Moonbeam'
Delphinium x *elatum*
Dianthus x *allwoodii* 'Doris' (pinks)
Digitalis grandiflora
Echinacea purpurea 'Magnus'
Echinacea purpurea 'White Swan'
Gaillardia x *grandiflora* 'Goblin'
Heliopsis helianthoides 'Summer Sun'
Hemerocallis 'Happy Returns' (daylily)
Hemerocallis 'Stella d'Oro' (daylily)
Leucanthemum x *superbum* cultivars (Shasta daisy)
Nepeta mussinii 'Blue Wonder' (catmint)
Nepeta sibirica (Siberian catmint)
Phlox paniculata cultivars (garden phlox)
Platycodon grandiflorus 'Sentimental Blue' (balloon flower)
Rosa cultivars
Salvia x *superba* cultivars
Scabiosa columbaria 'Butterfly Blue'
Verbena canadensis 'Homestead Purple'
Veronica alpina 'Goodness Grows'
Veronica spicata 'Blue Charm'
Veronica 'Sunny Border Blue'

Deadhead for aesthetics

Alchemilla mollis (lady's mantle)
Aruncus dioicus
Bergenia cordifolia
Campanula glomerata 'Superba'
Campanula lactiflora
Filipendula ulmaria 'Aurea'
Helenium autumnale 'Butterpat'
Hemerocallis cultivars (daylilies)
Heuchera cultivars

Hibiscus moscheutos 'Lord Baltimore'
Lamium maculatum
Monarda didyma
Physostegia virginiana
Platycodon grandiflorus 'Mariesii'
Pulmonaria longifolia ssp. *cevennensis*
Rodgersia aesculifolia
Solidago x 'Golden Baby'
Stachys byzantina

Deadhead to prevent "seeding about"

Achillea sibirica (yarrow)
Allium tuberosum (chives)
Aquilegia alpina (columbine)
Arabis caucasica 'Snowcap'
Asclepias tuberosa
Astrantia major
Brunnera macrophylla
Centaurea montana
Corydalis lutea
Euphorbia polychroma
Geranium sanguineum
Leucanthemum vulgare
Lychnis coronaria
Malva alcea 'Fastigiata'
Myosotis sylvatica

Nepeta (catmint)
Patrinia scabiosifolia
Phlox divaricata (woodland phlox)
Rudbeckia fulgida var. *sullivantii* 'Goldsturm'
Tanacetum parthenium 'Aureum'
Thalictrum aquilegiifolium (meadowrue)

Pinch for height control

In early June, pinch height in half!

Aster cultivars
Lavandula angustifolia 'Hidcote'
Monarda didyma cultivars (bee balm)
Perovskia atriplicifolia (Russian sage)
Phlox paniculata cultivars
Platycodon grandiflorus cultivars (balloon flower)
Physostegia virginiana cultivars (obedient plant)
Sedum x 'Autumn Joy'
Veronicastrum virginicum

Cut back to regenerate tired-looking plants

Bergenia cordifolia
Hemerocallis cultivars—after bloom
Iris sibirica
Lamium maculatum
Tradescantia cultivars (spiderwort)

Appendix A

Colored Foliage Bridges the Seasons of Bloom

Foliage interest is a result of color, texture, form, and light reflectance. You will want to take advantage of it for several reasons:

1. It lasts the entire growing season.
2. It provides a bridge of interest between bloom times.
3. It can blend flower colors or cool/hot combinations.
4. It adds winter interest.

Here are a few lists of different types of foliage plants to try in your garden. I think you'll be pleased—and maybe even surprised—at how much color you can achieve without a bloom!

COLORED FOLIAGE

Variegated

Athyrium nipponicum 'Pictum' (Japanese painted fern)
Lamium maculatum 'White Nancy' (spotted nettle)
Mentha suaveolens 'Variegata' (pineapple mint)
Polygonatum odoratum 'Variegatum' (variegated Solomon's seal)
Pulmonaria species (lungwort)

Silver

Achillea 'Moonshine' (yarrow)
Arabis caucasica 'Snowcap' (rock cress)
Artemisia ludoviciana 'Valerie Finnis'
Artemisia stelleriana 'Silver Brocade'
Lavandula angustifolia 'Hidcote'
Lychnis coronaria (rose campion)
Stachys byzantina (lamb's ear)
Veronica 'Minuet' (woolly speedwell)

Golden

Lamium maculatum 'Beedham's White' (spotted nettle)
Lysimachia nummularia 'Aureus' - moneywort
Origanum vulgare 'Aureum'
Tanacetum parthenium 'Aureum' (feverfew)

Blue

Allium senescens 'Glaucum' (ornamental onion)
Dianthus species (carnation/pinks)
Macleaya cordata (plume poppy)
Sedum species

Red/Purple

Cimicifuga ramosa 'Atropurpurea' (snakeroot)
Heuchera 'Plum Pudding' (coral bells)
Heuchera 'Smokey Rose' (coral bells)
Penstemon digitalis 'Husker's Red' (beard tongue)
Rosa glauca (*rubrifolia*) (red-foliaged rose)
Sedum x 'Ruby Glow'
Sedum x 'Vera Jameson'

Ornamental Grasses

Carex elata 'Bowles Golden' (gold-yellow)
Hakonechloa macra 'Aureola' (gold-yellow)
Helictotrichon sempervirens (blue)
Miscanthus sinensis 'Kaskade'
Miscanthus sinensis 'Malepartus'
Miscanthus sinensis 'Morning Light' (silver)
Miscanthus sinensis 'Nippon' (silver)
Miscanthus sinensis 'Purpurescens' (red)
Miscanthus sinensis 'Strictus' (yellow striped)
Panicum virgatum 'Rotstrahlbusch' (red)
Pennisetum alopecuroides (wheat)
Sorghastrum nutans 'Sioux Blue' (blue)

Ferns Provide Texture

Adiantum pedatum
Athyrium nipponicum 'Pictum'
Dryopteris marginalis (evergreen)
Onoclea sensibilis
Osmunda cinnamomea
Polystichum acrostichoides (evergreen)
Polystichum braunii (semi-evergreen)

Hostas

Glaucous, blue
Hosta fortunei 'Blue Angel'
Hosta 'Halcyon'
Hosta sieboldiana var. *elegans*

White-edged
Hosta 'Antioch'
Hosta fortunei 'Albo-marginata'
Hosta 'Gingko Craig'
Hosta 'Francee'

Golden
Hosta fortunei 'Gold Standard'
Hosta 'Piedmont Gold'
Hosta 'Sum and Substance'

Yellow-edged
Hosta sieboldiana 'Frances Williams'
Hosta 'Golden Tiara'
Hosta 'Shade Fanfare'
Hosta 'Wide Brim'

Green
Hosta 'Honeybells'
Hosta plantaginea (glossy)

Appendix B

Hostas by Color of Foliage

Hostas are the most adaptable shade perennials you can find. (If you can avoid slugs and deer!) To help you find the right hostas for your garden, I've listed them according to color, with brief descriptions for each.

Color	Name	Height/width	Description	Light	Use
Green	'Colossal'	24 x 36"	Dark green, large pointed	Shade to light sun	Specimen
	lancifolia	12 x 18"	Thin, dark green	Shade to 1/2 sun	Edger
	plantaginea	24 x 36"	Glossy heart; fragrant flower	Shade to part shade	Specimen
	'Royal Standard'	24 x 24"	Dark green; fragrant flower	Shade to full sun	Sun
Blue	*fortunei* 'Blue Angel'	36 x 36"	Blue-green	Shade to part sun	Specimen
	'Halcyon'	16 x 20"	Chalky blue	Shade to part sun	Edger
	'Krossa Regal'	30 x 24"	Upright, blue-gray	Shade to part shade	Specimen
	sieboldiana var. *elegans*	24 x 30"	Blue-gray	Shade to part shade	Specimen
Golden	'Gold Edger'	20 x 24"	Crinkled gold	Shade to 1/2 sun	Mid-border
	'Golden Scepter'	12 x 15"	Golden green	Part sun to light shade	Edger
	'Piedmont Gold'	36 x 50"	Huge yellow green	Shade to part sun	Background
	'Sum and Substance'	36 x 48"	Turns yellow with sun	Shade to 3/4 sun	Specimen
White variegated	'Antioch'	24 x 48"	Cascade of cream edge	Shade to light sun	Specimen
	fortunei 'Albo-marginata' ('Silver Crown')	18 x 30"	Green with white edge	Shade to light sun	Mid-border
	'Gingko Craig'	12 x 15"	Green with clear white edge	Shade to 1/2 sun	Edger
	'Patriot'	15 x 30"	Wider pure white margins	Part sun to light shade	Specimen
	'Stilleto'	6 x 8"	Narrow wavy with thin white	Shade to light shade	Edger
	undulata var. *albomarginata*	20 x 24"	Green with white edge	Shade to 1/2 sun	Groundcover
Yellow variegated	*fortunei* 'Aureo-marginata'	24 x 30"	Yellow edge	Shade to 3/4 sun	Groundcover
	fluctuans 'Sagae'	40 x 36"	Upright, blue-green with yellow edge	Shade to part sun	Background
	fortunei 'Gold Standard'	18 x 24"	Gold with dark green edge	1/4 to 3/4 sun	Groundcover
	'Golden Tiara'	12 x 8"	Light green with yellow edge	Shade to part sun	Edger
	'Kabitan'	8 x 10"	Yellow with green edge	Shade to 1/2 sun	Edger

Color	Name	Height/width	Description	Light	Use
	montana 'Aureo-marginata'	26 x 40"	Green with wide yellow edge	Shade to ¾ sun	Background
	'Shade Fanfare'	18 x 22"	Golden with cream edge	Shade to part sun	Groundcover
	'Wide Brim'	18 x 24"	Green with wide cream edge	Shade to ¾ sun	Specimen
	ventricosa 'Aureo-marginata'	18 x 24"	Wide cream edge	Part sun to light shade	Mid-border

Appendix C

Popular Mail-Order Astilbes:
A Guide to Color, Height, and Bloom Time

Flower Color	June	Mid-June to July	July	July to August	August
White	'Bumalda' 18–24" 'Deutschland' 20–24" 'Irrlicht' 18" 'Praecox Alba' 36" 'Queen of Holland' 24"	'Avalanche' 30" 'Bridal Veil' 24" 'Ellie' 18–24" 'Washington' 24–28"	'Gladstone' 20–24" 'Snowdrift' 24" 'White Perle' 28" 'William Buchanan' 6–8"	'Professor Van der Weilen' 36" 'White Gloria' 24–30"	'Darwin's Snow Sprite' 10–12" 'King Albert' 40"
Light Pink	'Erika' 30" 'Europa' 20"	'Grete Pungel' 40"	'America' 20" 'Peach Blossom' 24–30"	'Hennie Graafland' 15–20" 'Inshriach Pink' 12" 'Jacqueline' 28" 'Sprite' 12"	'Finale' 15–18" 'Rosea' 15"
Medium to Dark Pink		'Bremen' 24" 'Bonn' 20" 'Cattleya' 36" 'Rheinland' 24–30"	'Bressingham Beauty' 30–36" 'Intermezzo' 9–12" 'Ostrich Plume' 36" 'Vision in Pink' 18"	'Anita Pfeifer' 24–30" 'Aphrodite' 12–15" 'Dunkellachs' 18–24" 'Federsee' 24" 'Perkeo' 6–8"	'Bronze Elegans' 12" 'Darwin's Dream' 10"
Lilac to Purple/Rose	'Mars' 24"	'Amethyst' 24–30" 'Mainz' 18–24"	'Harmony' 45" 'Maggie Daley' 28"	'Jo Ophorst' 36" 'Raspberry Pink' 18" 'Veronica Klose' 16" 'Visions' 12–14"	*chinensis* 'Pumila' 8–10" *chinensis* 'Purpurkerze' 36" *chinensis* 'Superba' 36–40"

Flower Color	June	Mid-June to July	July	July to August	August
Light Red	'Vesuvius' 24"	'Fire' 30" 'Venus Summers' 24"	'Red Sentinel' 20–24" 'Montgomery' 24"	'Granaat' 24" 'Serenade' 14"	
Dark Red	'Koln' 15–20"	'Fanal' 18–24" 'Glow' 18" 'Red Light' 24–28" 'Spinell' 30"	'Etna' 24"		

Appendix D

Select Daylilies: A Guide to Color, Height, and Bloom Time

Flower Color	June	Mid-June to July	July	July to August	August
Orange	'Bertie Ferris' 18–20"	fulva 36–40"	'Raging Tiger' 25"	'Baltimore Oriole' 26"	
		'Sparkling Orange' 34"	'Song Sparrow' 24"	'Rocket City' 30"	
				'Sombrero Way' 24"	
Peach/Melon, Coral	'Sirocco' 24–28"	'Louise Manelis' 18"	'Frances Fay' 32"	'Elaine Strutt' 36"	
		'Peach Fairy' 26"	'Toyland' 24"		
Gold	'Mary Todd' 26"	'Stella d'Oro' 28" (repeats)	'Golden Pond' 25"	'Golden Prize' 26"	'Radiant Beams' 22–24"
Yellow	'Carolyn Criswell' 24"	'Buttercurls' 28"	'Big Bird' 36"	'Buttered Popcorn' 32"	'Green Flutter' 32"
	flava 24"	'Eenie Weenie' 10"	'Butterpat' 18–20"	'Northbrook Star' 36"	'Olin Criswell' 30"
		'Happy Returns' 16" (repeats)	'Electric' 24"	'Statuesque' 60"	'Yellow Stone' 36"
		'Penny's Worth' 14–16"	'Hyperion' 36"	'Tetrina's Daughter' 48–52"	
Near white		'Dad's Best White' 24-28"	'Arctic Snow' 23"	'White Perfection' 30"	
		'Gentle Shepherd' 29"	'Ice Carnival' 24–28"		
		'Pandora's Box' 19"	'Joan Senior' 20–24"		
Pink/Rose	'Dardenella' 26"	'Baby Talk' 18–22"	'Bama Music' 24–28"	'Bonnie Barbara Allen' 28"	'Hall's Pink' 20"
	'Pink Merriment' 23"	'Mini Pearl' 16"	'Catherine Woodbury' 36"	'Fairy Tale Pink' 24"	'Last Picture Show' 26"
		'Pink Lavender Appeal' 26–30"	'Cherry Lace' 36"	'Cherry Cheeks' 24–30"	'Tender Love' 18–22"

Flower Color	June	Mid-June to July	July	July to August	August
		'Siloam Baby Talk' 15"	'Naomi Ruth' 16"	'Hello Dolly' 42"	
			'Pink Damask' 32–36"		
Red	'Scarlet Orbit' 22"	'Baja' 26"	'Buzz Bomb' 20"	'Red Pinocchio' 24"	
		'Christmas Is' 20–24"	'Chicago Fire' 34"	'Stop Sign' 29"	
			'Christmas Carol' 34"	'Wide Wide World' 34"	
Wine/Purple	'Chicago Royal Robe' 25"	'Intoxication' 28"	'Cedar Waxwing' 30"	'Grape Velvet' 24"	
	'Little Wine Cup' 24"	'Little Grapette' 10–12"	'Darius' 22"	'Prairie Blue Eyes' 24–28"	
	'Zinfadel' 26"	'Royal Palace Purple' 30"	'Summer Wine' 24"		

Appendix E

Perennials Least Affected by Deer- and Rabbit-Browse

Browsing by deer and rabbits is one of the biggest problems in the garden. Gardeners have tried many tricks to fool these pesky animals like fencing, bird netting, and all sorts of smelly concoctions—even noise-makers and light. One client even sprayed her garden with Right Guard deodorant every evening to fool the deer with this human scent. Whatever works for you! And you can find a very humorous discussion by Joyce Schillen called "Bambi Does Breakfast . . ." on the Internet at www.gardenpages.com/bambi.html.

I think it helps to know the plants that these animals are particularly fond of. Deer seem to love yews, euonymus, daylilies, border phlox, and hostas, and they'll graze these plants down to their nubs. Rabbits, on the other hand, prefer asters, dianthus, creeping phlox, and lilies. They can also do great damage to roses in the winter.

Using just the perennials in this book, I have created a list of perennials that have been the least-likely targets of deer- and rabbit-browse. I would also suggest that perennials with aromatic foliage (and these are often herbs) act as deterrents. But this should be tempered with the thought that this may not be true in your garden and that the animals will eat anything when hungry! Experience is the best teacher.

Achillea sibirica
Achillea x 'Anthea'
Achillea 'Moonshine'
Aconitum x *cammarum* 'Newry Blue'
Aconitum carmichaelii
Actaea rubra
Adiantum pedatum
Alchemilla mollis
Allium aflatunense 'Purple Sensation'
Allium christophii
Allium senescens 'Glaucum'
Allium tuberosum
Amsonia tabernaemontana
Anaphalis triplinervis 'Summer Snow'
Anemone blanda
Anemone x *hybrida* 'Honorine Jobert'
Anemone sylvestris
Anemone vitifolia 'Robustissima'
Anemonella thalictroides
Aquilegia alpina
Aquilegia canadensis
Aquilegia canadensis 'Corbett'
Aguilegia longissima 'Maxistar'
Arabis caucasica 'Snowcap'
Arisaema triphyllum
Artemisia lactiflora

Artemisia ludoviciana 'Valerie Finnis'
Artemisia stelleriana 'Silver Brocade'
Astilbe x *arendsii* 'Bressingham Beauty'
Astilbe x *arendsii* 'Deutschland'
Astilbe x *arendsii* 'Fanal'
Astilbe chinensis 'Pumila'
Astilbe japonica 'Red Sentinel'
Astilbe japonica 'Rheinland'
Astilbe simplicifolia 'Praecox Alba'
Astilbe simplicifolia 'Sprite'
Astrantia major
Athyrium filix-femina
Athyrium nipponicum 'Pictum'
Bergenia cordifolia
Brunnera macrophylla
Camassia leichtlinii
Campanula carpatica 'Deep Blue Clips'
Campanula glomerata 'Superba'
Campanula lactiflora
Carex elata 'Bowles Golden'
Caryopteris x *clandonensis* 'Longwood Blue'
Centaurea montana
Ceratostigma plumbaginoides
Cimicifuga ramosa 'Atropurpurea'
Cimicifuga ramosa 'Hillside Black Beauty'
Cimicifuga simplex 'White Pearl'

Clematis hybrids
Corydalis lutea
Dicentra spectabilis
Dicentra formosa 'Luxuriant'
Digitalis grandiflora
Digitalis purpurea
Epimedium 'Crimson'
Epimedium x *versicolor* 'Sulphureum'
Eupatorium coelestinum
Eupatorium maculatum 'Gateway'
Eupatorium rugosum 'Chocolate'
Euphorbia corollata
Euphorbia dulcis 'Chameleon'
Euphorbia epithymoides 'Polychroma'
Euphorbia myrsinites
Ferns
Filipendula rubra
Filipendula ulmaria 'Aurea'
Gaillardia x *grandiflora* 'Goblin'
Geranium x *cantabrigiense* 'Biokovo'
Geranium maculatum
Geranium x *magnificum*
Geranium sanguineum var. *striatum*
Geranium wallichianum 'Buxton's Variety'
Helenium autumnale 'Butterpat'
Helictotrichon sempervirens
Helleborus orientalis
Hemerocallis cultivars (resistant to rabbits only)
Herbs
Iris cristata
Iris pallida 'Argentea-variegata'
Iris sibirica 'Caesar's Brother'
Iris tectorum
Kalimeris pinnatifida
Kirengeshoma palmata
Lamium maculatum 'Beedham's White'
Lamium maculatum 'White Nancy'
Leucanthemum x *superbum* 'Aglaia'
Leucanthemum x *superbum* 'Ryan's White'
Leucanthemum x *superbum* 'Snowcap'
Leucanthemum vulgare
Leucojum aestivum 'Gravetye Giant'
Lychnis coronaria

Lysimachia clethroides
Lysimachia nummularia 'Aureus'
Lysimachia punctata
Malva alcea 'Fastigiata'
Miscanthus sinensis 'Kaskade'
Miscanthus sinensis 'Malepartus'
Miscanthus sinensis 'Morning Light'
Miscanthus sinensis 'Nippon'
Miscanthus sinensis 'Purpurescens'
Miscanthus sinensis 'Strictus'
Monarda didyma 'Gardenview Scarlet'
Monarda didyma 'Marshall's Delight'
Monarda didyma 'Raspberry Wine'
Muscari armeniacum
Myosotis sylvatica
Narcissus cyclamineus 'February Gold'
Nepeta mussinii 'Blue Wonder'
Onoclea sensibilis
Origanum vulgare 'Aureum'
Osmunda cinnamomea
Paeonia officinalis 'Flame'
Panicum virgatum 'Rotstrahlbusch'
Patrinia scabiosifolia
Pennisetum alopecuroides
Penstemon digitalis 'Husker's Red'
Perovskia atriplicifolia
Phlomis fruticosa
Polygonatum commutatum
Polygonatum odoratum 'Variegatum'
Polystichum acrostichoides
Polystichum braunii
Pulmonaria longifolia ssp. *cevennensis*
Rudbeckia fulgida var. *sullivantii* 'Goldsturm'
Rudbeckia nitida 'Herbstsonne'
Salvia verticillata 'Purple Rain'
Salvia x *superba* 'Blue Hill'
Salvia x *superba* 'May Night'
Saponaria ocymoides 'Max Frei'
Scabiosa columbaria 'Butterfly Blue'
Scilla sibirica
Sedum x 'Autumn Joy'
Sedum x 'Ruby Glow'
Silphium perfoliatum

Sorghastrum nutans 'Sioux Blue'
Sporobolus heterolepsis
Stachys byzantina
Stachys byzantina 'Helene von Stein'
Stachys macrantha 'Superba'
Stachys officinalis 'Alba'
Thalictrum aquilegiifolium 'Album'
Thalictrum flavum 'Glaucum'

Thalictrum rochebrunianum
Tiarella 'Iron Butterfly'
Tiarella wherryi
Tradescantia virginiana 'Concord Grape'
Tradescantia x *andersoniana* 'Zwanenberg Blue'
Trillium grandiflorum (resistant to rabbits only)
Trollius chinensis (resistant to rabbits only)
Verbena canadensis 'Homestead Purple'

Appendix F

A Few Mail-Order Catalogs

Ambergate Gardens
8730 County Road 43
Chaska, MN 55318-9358
(612) 443-2248

Arrowhead Alpines
P.O. Box 857
Fowlersville, MI 48836
(517) 223-3581

W. Atlee Burpee
300 Park Avenue
Warminster, PA 18974
(800) 888-1447
www.burpee.com

Kurt Bluemel Inc.
2740 Greene Lane
Baldwin, MD 21013
(410) 557-7229

Bluestone Perennials
7231 Middle Ridge Road
Madison, OH 44057
(800) 852-5243

Brent and Becky's Bulbs
7463 Heath Trail
Gloucester, VA 23061
(804) 693-3966

Busse Gardens
13579 10th Street N.W.
Ckato, MN 55321-9426
(320) 286-2654

Canyon Creek Nursery
3527 Dry Creek Road
Oroville, CA 95965
(530) 533-2166

Collector's Nursery
16804 N.E. 102nd Avenue
Battle Ground, WA 98604
(360) 574-3832

Gardens Alive
5100 Schenley Place
Lawrenceburg, IN 47025
(812) 537-8650
(Organic supplies)

Gardener's Supply
128 Intervale Road
Burlington, VT 05401
(802) 660-3500
(Organic supplies and tools)

Heirloom Old Garden Roses
24062 NE Riverside Drive
St. Paul, OR 97137
(503) 538-1576

Heronswood Nursery Ltd.
7530 288th Street NE
Kingston, WA 98346
(206) 297-4127

Jackson & Perkins
2518 S. Pacific Highway
Medford, OR 97501
(541) 776-2000
www.jacksonperkins.com

Klehm Nursery
4201 N. Duncan Road
Champaign, IL 61821
(800) 553-3715

McClure & Zimmerman
P.O. Box 368
108 W. Winnebago
Friesland, WI 53935
(414) 326-4220

Mellinger's
2310 W. South Range Road
North Lima, OH 44452-9731
(216) 549-9861

Milaegar's Gardens
4838 Douglas Avenue
Racine, WI 53402
(800) 669-9956
www.garden.com

Picadilly Farm LLC
1971 Whippoorwill Road
Bishop, GA 30621
(706) 769-6516

Plant Delights Nursery
9241 Sauls Road
Raleigh, NC 27603
(919) 772-4794
www.plantdel.com

Prairie Nursery
P.O. Box 306
Westfield, WI 53964
(608) 297-3679

Robyn's Nest
7802 N.E. 63rd Street
Vancouver, WA 98662
(206) 256-7399

Roslyn Nursery
211 Burrs Lane
Dix Hills, NY 11746
(516) 643-9347

Shady Oaks Nursery
112 10th Avenue, SE
Waseca, MN 56093
(800) 504-8006

Siskiyou Rare Plant Nursery
2825 Cummings Road
Medford, OR 97501
(503) 772-6846
(Alpine and rock garden plants)

Terra Nova Nurseries Inc.
12162 S.W. Scholls Ferry Road
Tigard, OR 97223
www.terranovnurseries.com
(wholesale only)

Thompson & Morgan
P.O. Box 1308
Jackson, NJ 08527-0308
(800) 274-7333
www.thompson-morgan.com

Andre Viette Farm and Nursery
Route 1, Box 16
Fischerville, VA 22939
(540) 943-2315

Wayside Gardens
1 Garden Lane
Hodges, SC 29695
(800) 845-1124

Well-Sweep Herb Farm
317 Mt. Bethel Road
Port Murray, NJ 07865
(980) 852-5390

White Flower Farm
Route 63
Litchfield, CN 06759
(800) 503-9624
www.whiteflowerfarm.com

Appendix G

Plant Societies

The best way to learn about gardening with perennials is to visit as many different public and private gardens as you can. Look for ideas, combinations and perennials new to you. Note what you like and how they are used because these can be reinterpreted in your garden. I call it "stealing with your eyes"!

Be sure to ask the gardener any questions—find out about the plants' problems and care firsthand. Continuous learning is an important part of planning for continuous bloom.

Plant societies, botanical gardens, extension services, and garden clubs can be invaluable sources of information and learning. Some produce newsletters, journals, or magazines. Most have meetings and classes or lectures with opportunities to learn from fellow gardeners and experts.

The following list of plant societies should give you a great place to start learning.

The Cottage Garden Society
Clive Lane
Brandon, Ravenshall, Betley
Cheshire CW3 9BH
England

American Daffodil Society Inc.
Naomi Liggett
4126 Winfield Road
Columbus, OH 43220
www.mc.edu/~adswww

The Delphinium Society
Mrs. Shirley E. Bassett
Takakkaw, Ice House Wood
Oxted, Surrey RH8 9DW
England

American Fern Society
David P. Lellinger
U.S. National Herbarium
NHB #166
Smithsonian Institution
Washington, DC 20560
www.visualink.com/fern

Garden Conservancy
P.O. Box 219
Coldspring, NY 10516
www.gardenconservancy.com

The National Gardening Association
180 Flynn Avenue
Burlington, VT 05401
www2.garden.org/nga

International Geranium Society
P.O. Box 92734
Pasadena, CA 91109-2734

Hardy Plant Society—Great Britain
Pam Adams
Little Orchard, Great Comberton
Pershore, Worcestershire WR10 3DP
England

Hardy Plant Society—Connecticut
Ken Twombly
163 Barn Hill Road
Monroe, CT 06468

Hardy Plant Society—Michigan
Julie Cromer
29720 Wildbrook Drive
Southfield, MI 48034

Hardy Plant Society—Mid Atlantic Group
Nancy Greenwood
645 Harwick Road
Wayne, PA 19087

Hardy Plant Society—Wisconsin
Frank R. Greer
925 Waban Hill
Madison, WI 53711

Springer, Lauren. *The Undaunted Gardener*. Golden, CO: Fulcrum Publishing, 1994.

Still, Steven M. *Herbaceous Ornamental Plants*. Champaign, IL: Stipes Publishing Company, 1994.

Thomas, Graham Stuart. *Perennial Garden Plants*. Portland, OR: Sagapress, 1990.

Time-Life Books. *The Big Book of Flower Gardening*. Alexandria, VA: Time-Life Books, 1996.

Wilson, Jim. *Landscaping with Herbs*. New York, NY: Houghton Mifflin, 1994.

Woods, Christopher. *Encyclopedia of Perennials: A Gardener's Guide*. New York: Facts on File, 1992.

Wyman, Donald. *Wyman's Gardening Encyclopedia*. New York: MacMillan, 1977.

Index to Botanical Names

Index to Common Names